Tribal Modern

The publisher gratefully acknowledges the generous support of the Ahmanson Foundation Humanities Endowment Fund of the University of California Press Foundation.

Tribal Modern

Branding New Nations in
the Arab Gulf

miriam cooke

UNIVERSITY OF CALIFORNIA PRESS
Berkeley   Los Angeles   London

University of California Press, one of the most distinguished university presses in the
United States, enriches lives around the world by advancing scholarship in the
humanities, social sciences, and natural sciences. Its activities are supported by the
UC Press Foundation and by philanthropic contributions from individuals and
institutions. For more information, visit www.ucpress.edu.

University of California Press
Berkeley and Los Angeles, California

University of California Press, Ltd.
London, England

Library of Congress Cataloging-in-Publication Data

Cooke, Miriam.
   Tribal modern : branding new nations in the Arab Gulf / Miriam Cooke.
      pages   cm
   ISBN 978-0-520-28009-0 (hardback)—ISBN 978-0-520-28010-6 (paperback)
   1. Ethnology—Persian Gulf States.   2. Persian Gulf States—Social life and
customs.   3. Tribes—Persian Gulf States.   I. Title.
   GN640.C66 2014
   306.09536—dc23

                                                                2013019649

Manufactured in the United States of America

23 22 21 20 19 18 17 16 15 14
10 9 8 7 6 5 4 3 2 1

In keeping with a commitment to support environmentally responsible and
sustainable printing practices, UC Press has printed this book on Rolland Enviro100,
a 100% post-consumer fiber paper that is FSC certified, deinked, processed chlorine-
free, and manufactured with renewable biogas energy. It is acid-free and EcoLogo
certified.

For Muhammad Àli Àbdullah and DD

CONTENTS

Introduction

Bombay. February 1973.

I was running out of money. After months on the road, I was tired of traveling. Busing and hitching across Europe through Turkey to Afghanistan through the Khyber Pass and Rawalpindi to Katmandu and down to Goa for Christmas and Trivandrum for New Year's Eve had finally slaked my wanderlust. Instead of Bali, I decided to return to Bombay and then home. Home in oh-so-far-away England.

With little money left, my only option was the "human cargo ship." These vessels of misery left Bombay when they had filled with Indian laborers bound for the Arab Gulf. The accelerating production of oil drove the demand for migrant workers. South Asia supplied them. More and more ships were filling and leaving. At the port of Bombay, I met with the ship's captain and handed over my twenty pounds sterling to cover the cost of my trip to the Iranian port of Khorramshahr. Before setting sail, I signed a document accepting the conditions of travel: no doctor on board.

For ten nights, I slept in the black bowels of the ship. My hammock was squeezed between other hammocks, packed with women and screaming, puking babies. It was hard to sleep. Morning brought relief. Bleary-eyed, we climbed the stairs out of the stinking hold and onto the deck where we lined up for breakfast. Stewards slopped curry into our outstretched bowls. Lunch and dinner were the same. The only break from the monotony of potato curry was afternoon tea, sweet and milky, with Marie biscuits.

After passing through the Strait of Hormuz, the ship stopped at the various towns dotting the Arab Gulf coast. We anchored for a few hours to disembark passengers in their assigned port of call. Under guard, they were herded down the gangplank and quickly separated into small groups before vanishing into the maze of narrow streets beyond the port. Since I was the only non-Indian passenger and not likely to escape, the captain made an exception to the rule that no one could leave the docked ship. With the sailors I wandered around the various ports for a few hours.

The only place I really remember is Dubai. The British, after presiding over the Gulf region for over one hundred and fifty years, had withdrawn two years earlier. They had left little trace of their presence. This dusty town of one- and two-story mud buildings was at the time "the largest conurbation in the region" and the "business capital of the Trucial coast" with a population of over 100,000, half being foreigners (Davidson 2008, 68–69). The only "tourist attraction" I recall was a Russian hospital. It was highly recommended, and so I joined a couple of the sailors who were on their first trip to the Gulf. The car wound its way through the streets and then quickly out into the desert. There it was, a large, glass, empty edifice. Rumor had it that those who entered did not leave alive. We kept our distance.

Bleak and colorless though it was, Dubai had seemed uncannily familiar.

. . .

Dubai. December 2008.

About to land in Dubai International Airport, I wondered if I would again experience those intimations of a previous incarnation. Flying over the city, I knew I wouldn't.

I entered the huge, glass airport that serves as one of the busiest hubs in the world. Teeming with people, it felt like Heathrow or JFK. After a long wait for the luggage, I caught a taxi and asked the driver to take me to the Palm Jumeirah and then through the downtown. Happy to comply, he drove me around the man-made island shaped like a palm tree with the monstrous Atlantis Hotel looming at the end. Next, we passed the seven-star, sail-shaped Burj al-'Arab Hotel. It boasts the world's highest tennis court that, at 211 meters, serves also as a helipad. From the coast, we drove inland and passed Knowledge Village, Dubai Internet City, Dubai Media City Annex, and Mall of the Emirates, where the pinnacle of the world's largest indoor ski slope towers above the commercial complex. Heavy traffic slowed to a crawl through the six-lane highway separating the two sides of the Sheikh Zayed Road known as Dubai's Fifth Avenue. Most stunning of all was the 828-meter high Burj Khalifa, the world's tallest building in the shape of a rocket.[1]

Finally, we entered an older part of town where I alighted and walked through a maze of alleys to the Xva Art boutique hotel where I had booked a room for two nights. A traditional house converted into an art gallery-cum-hotel, it is located in Bastakia, a restored heritage area inaccessible to cars. The hotel was a two-minute walk from the Khor, or Creek, a bustling hive of activity where I had landed all those years ago. Bastakia's romantic wind towers and hushed, narrow lanes flanked by high, white, windowless walls allowed the imagination to roam to a time in the past when Arabs, Persians, and Indians traded and traveled from there to all parts of the Indian Ocean.

Nothing in this vertical city with its fantasy architecture recalled the place I had briefly visited in 1973. In December 2008, I found myself less in a place than in a condition. Architect and professor at the American University in Sharjah, George Katodrytis captures the surreal mood of Dubai when he writes "the 'thrill' of the urban voyage is quickly giving way to banality and exhaustion... The city tends to be everywhere and nowhere at the same time, because it has no urban center or core... Dubai may be considered the emerging prototype for the 21st century: prosthetic and nomadic oases presented as isolated cities" (Katodrytis 2005, 42, 43).

Dubai, like the six other emirates of the United Arab Emirates (UAE)—Ajman, Umm al-Quwain, Ras al-Khaima, Fujeira, Sharjah, Abu Dhabi—and Qatar, resembles Shanghai and Las Vegas more than the dusty town that had surprised me thirty-five years earlier. Dubai has become the icon of a world in transition. With a population that has increased twentyfold and skyscrapers blanketing miles upon miles of what used to be desert, Dubai may be more over-the-top than other Gulf cities, but just below the surface, the mix of timeless desert and helter-skelter modern is everywhere the same: camel races and Lamborghinis; falcon markets and indoor ski slopes; camping in the desert and Jeeps "bashing" dunes. Beyond the endless pursuit of fun and profit, the same question must be asked of Dubai and its Gulf neighbors: how do real people live in such unreal places?

. . .

In the 1970s one of the hottest, most forbidding regions of the world burst onto the international stage. Unimaginable wealth had suddenly accrued to desperately poor tribes in the UAE, Qatar, Bahrain and Kuwait. Successors to the fishing and pearling shaikhdoms made destitute in the early twentieth century by competition with the Japanese cultured pearl industry, ultra-modern petro-cities sprouted up out of the Arabian deserts and along the Arab Gulf coast. The discovery and exploitation of oil in the mid-twentieth century allowed Gulf Arab rulers to dream big, very big. The national project was to turn tribal shaikhdoms into world hubs for transnational flows of people, goods, and capital. Tribal leaders became modern monarchs of tiny political entities, each carved out of shared tribal territory and identical histories.

Now, in the twenty-first century, they are fashioning independent, modern nation-states with historically and politically differentiated societies. Yet sameness prevails. In the attempt to highlight national uniqueness, icons dot the cityscape and especially the ubiquitous Corniche, a prestigious strip of reclaimed land lining each nation-state's stretch of the Gulf coast. These national symbols, however, derive from the pre-oil days: an oryx, a pearl, a coffee pot, a dhow or an incense burner, and importantly, a falcon. Representing the Prophet Muhammad's tribe of the Quraysh, the falcon telegraphs tribal aristocracy. Sharing history and geography, these countries perforce share the same symbols from their common past.

Gulf Arab citizens are a rare sighting except in malls, where they stroll majestically through air-conditioned spaces. Indians, Sri Lankans, Filipinos, Indonesians, Malays, Burmese, and Europeans scurry past tall, thin women elegant in their black cloaks, or `abayas, and their hair piled high under the black scarves, or *shaylas*. Foreigners step aside careful not to get in the way of tall young men walking hand in hand, their sparkling white gowns, or *thawbs*[2] crisp. Constantly adjusting their starched white headdress, the *gutra*, and nonchalantly throwing the tips of the scarf over their head, they glance at their reflection in shop windows to check the effect.

These women in black and men in white are the scions of tribes who knew no roof but the sky and the goat-hair tent. From pre-Islamic times, poets sang a life of travel from oasis to oasis, where they named each dune according to its shape and resilience, each stage in a camel's life, and each shade of its hair. Each plant, each wind, each cloud had a name to define its moment in time. In the space between the hard-packed sand and the soft sand that the zephyr breezes blew back and forth, the sixth-century tribal prince poet Imrul Qais detected the trace of the encampment where he remembered his forbidden love. The tribe learned of their tryst and they took her away, far away. And yet, no matter how much the wind stirs up the sands the trace remains and the poet will go mad with longing. Such pre-Islamic odes to lost loves fill the canon of Arabic literature.

These poets of ancient Arabia, whose intimacy with nature allowed them to wander freely where outsiders could not survive a day, have inspired a new generation of oral poets. They are reviving desert tropes to address and even welcome new realities. In the following fragment of a poem by Bakhut al-Mariyah, the desert and the sky, representing the traditional, tribal past and the modern present, are intertwined:

> The passenger of that which is in heavenly space walks by the
>   movement of
> Its sound, because of its speed, throwing it behind
> It leaves the airport in the forenoon
> Passing the camels' herdsman, who has not left his home.
> It crosses the passengers of the Dodge before Dumwat, cutting
>   across the
> Red Sulba and the encampment below.
>
> al-Ghadeer 2009, 156

The plane, recalling the roc of *Arabian Nights* fame, crosses time and space in the blink of an eye. Saudi Bakhut al-Mariyah juxtaposes the tribal and the modern in what is by now a familiar trope. A Bedouin woman looking up from the encampment to the plane, like this image of Bedouin men riding their camels into a hypermodern city to celebrate a special event, emblematize the tradition-modernity clash (see Figure 1).

How, some wonder, can such tribal people negotiate the clashing complexities of our modern world?

In addressing this question, *Tribal Modern* challenges its binary assumptions. The tribal and the modern must be thought of together. I argue that one must look below the surface of these newly rich desert societies to find the different meanings that attach to the appearance of the nonmodern, in this case the tribal. My argument throughout this book will be that the tribal is not the traditional and certainly not the primitive.[3]

Figure 1. Tribes, camels, and skyscrapers.

This statement calls for elaboration. Let's turn briefly to the December 1984 New York Museum of Modern Art (MoMA) exhibition entitled " 'Primitivism' in 20th Century Art: Affinity of the Tribal and the Modern."[4] A spectacular display of non-Western artefacts alongside works of Western modernist art, the exhibition sparked a craze for all things primitive/tribal—the terms were used interchangeably during the 1980s and 1990s. Widely reviewed at the time, the exhibition attracted negative reviews from some scholars. In "Doctor, Lawyer, Indian Chief: 'Primitivism' in Modern Art at the Museum of Modern Art" (*Artforum*, November 1984), Thomas McEvilly derided the show's Eurocentric, colonialist, even racist "privileging of European art over the indigenously tribal arts . . . as sources of the visual forms and motifs that informed key European Modernist painters." Particularly offensive to McEvilly was "the mainstream practice of exhibiting and discussing non-Western production without naming the artists or dating their arts." Tribal art became mere "footnotes to Modernist production."[5]

In *The Predicament of Culture* (1988), anthropologist James Clifford provided his critique in the chapter on "Histories of the Tribal and the Modern." The title would lead the reader to expect a consistent analysis of the tribal modern. Instead, the tribal stands in for people and places outside the West. Contra the MoMA curators' claim that the tribal is the past, Clifford asserts that tribes are part of the present, but it is the non-Western present. He refuses any "essential affinity between tribal and modern or even a coherent modernist attitude toward the primitive but rather the restless desire and power of the modern West to collect the world" (196). Note the way he elides the difference between the tribal and the primitive in a single sentence. The point he makes is that the tribal/primitive cultural context within which these objects have been produced disappears in the ahistorical formal mix-and-match agenda of the MoMA exhibition. Tribes/primitive people, he insists, are alive and well and not part of a vanishing world. However, they are also not part of the modern Western world. With their complex cultures they are of a different order from the modern that Clifford assumes to be Western. The tribe in the MoMA version is a chronotope whose time is the past and whose place is the non-West; in Clifford's version the time of the tribe chronotope is the present, although, like the place of MoMA's tribes, its topos is the non-West.[6]

The tribal in *Tribal Modern* is far from that anthropological primitive—whether historicized or not—located beyond the reach of Western modernity. The tribal as it appears in the Arab Gulf today is integral to the modern; it constitutes a crucial element in the Gulf's modernity. The tribal was repressed in the middle of the twentieth century because oil imperialists and their local agents considered it a hindrance to modernization, but the tribal is making a comeback in the twenty-first century. In its return, the tribal signals racial privilege, social status, and exclusive entitlement to a share in national profits. Indeed, the rubbing up of the tribal against the modern in today's Gulf states does not represent a *clash* of conflicting values, but, rather, the *desired effect* of common aspirations. This effect will be analyzed through the lens of the *barzakh*, a term denoting undiluted convergence. It derives from the Qur'an where it depicts simultaneous mixing and separation in two dimensions: metaphysical and physical. The undiluted convergences between this life and the hereafter and between salt and sweet water I will amplify in chapter four.

Examining the culture of the United Arab Emirates, Qatar, Bahrain, and Kuwait, *Tribal Modern* traces the emergence of a national brand that combines the spectacle of tribal and modern identities and cultures. The brand is widely visible yet poorly understood, and the goal of this book is to present the brand in such a way that it compels attention to the absolute simultaneity and compatibility of the tribal and the modern without privileging one over the other.

The outcome of my research goes against the grain of popular thinking and media hype. Highly stigmatized, the region tends to be considered as either tribal or modern; in other words, it is either backward tribal with a thin, modern veneer or failed modern because of tribal residue. Refer back to Figure 1 of the Dukhan Camel Club procession about to greet Qatar's Emir on December 3, 2010, upon his return from Zurich, where Qatar was awarded the 2022 World Cup. People to whom I have shown this image have shrugged, saying that there is nothing new here. Some see only the camels and the dhows, others only the starchitect skyline; for most, this juxtaposition provides proof of the cognitive dissonance between the tribal and the modern. But to begin to understand the culture of the Gulf and to appreciate what is new and different in it, we must see how the modern and the tribal, the high-rises and the tribal regalia, converge, each reinforcing the other.

The category of tribe/tribal projects something new and crucial in the twenty-first century. A racialized idea that catalyzes a distinctively modern identity for Gulf Arab citizens, tribal designation distinguishes native citizens from others close to them, the majority international community of workers. It provides a cultural, social, and political resource for young Gulf Arab elites, seeking to reconnect with grandparents who experienced cyclical austerity and constant movement across vast borderless zones. Only the tribal bond allows Gulf youth to comprehend the dignified poverty and the restlessness of their ancestors. They are redefining the tribal for their times and in their own lives. Like the Medicis in sixteenth-century Italy and the Vanderbilts in nineteenth-century America, the Arab Gulf tribes in the twenty-first century are asserting both tribal superiority and family privilege.

These aspirations occlude elements from their immediate and distant history. Tribes are said to have always existed beyond foreign influence, and many claim that foreigners are new in the region. Yet, history records millennia of interaction across the Indian Ocean. The latest foreigners to come to the Gulf were the Americans, whose arrival in the 1930s Saudi novelist 'Abd al-Rahman Munif vividly describes in his 1984 *Cities of Salt*. Indispensable for the economy, foreigners are considered a threat to be marginalized today and erased from yesterday. In chapter one, I consider the suppression of transnational connections in the past. Further, today's foreigners—Asian workers along with American and European "educated cosmopolitans"—are represented as new and, in the case of the laborers, contaminating. In the newly cosmopolitan cities, the less said about the region's heterogeneous past the better.

How does the elite tribal minority hold on to its privileged status? The first step is to assert unique right to citizenship and exclusive entitlement to national wealth. Only those who have inhabited these lands since time immemorial, namely the tribes, can claim that right. Nation building on tribal territories has turned tribe into race into nation. The next step involves fabricating immediately recognizable identities to differentiate Gulf Arabs from the mass of foreign workers. Chapter two discusses the recent emphasis on pure tribal identities and lineages that draw an unbreachable line between native citizen and visiting foreigner. With the establishment of Gulf nation-states, new national borders were drawn. In many cases, they cut through tribal territory so that today the tribal and the national compete in shaping "authentic" identities. Tribal purity, the *sine qua non* of citizenship, is maintained through marriages arranged within the racialized norms of tribal equivalence and compatibility, and impeccable genealogies preserve the veneer of tribal purity.

Students in a class I was teaching in fall 2010 at the Virginia Commonwealth University–Qatar conducted surveys on marriage and tribal status. Its results demonstrate how pervasive yet complex is the prestige conferred by tribal lineage and consequent status. The chapter ends with an exposé of the connection between DNA and money. Birthright, genetics, and consanguinity—all provide the crucial building blocks in a citizens' rights discourse that celebrates tribal origins.

Analysis of nation building reveals the constructedness of pure tribal blood and traces how it has changed into the idea of the tribe. Chapter three discusses this process. But is this a novel development? I argue that it is not. I explore the production of tribal lineages in a rapidly changing political and economic climate. The tribal, the national, and the modern are inextricably bound to one another. The transformations of tribal ties and genealogies into race and then into class—especially urban cosmopolitan class—become critical for citizenship. The emergence of the privileged national citizen reveals the interdependence and the reciprocity of the tribal and the modern.

The inflated yet flexible idea of the tribe shapes a distinctive national brand that broadcasts class, race, and power. Every brand needs a slogan. Authenticity, often a synonym for the tribal, is the oft-repeated slogan that shapes the new Gulf Arab brand. Chapter four looks at the creation of the tribal modern brand as a new space where the potential for dynamic interaction is released. This brand brings together contradictory states in a broader border that I call the *barzakh*, an untranslatable term signifying undiluted convergence, the simultaneous processes of mixing and separation. Contradictions stand in the borderlands, bringing together and separating the symbolic tribal and the material modern. Resisting resolution, these contradictions spiral into new forms of productive branding. Gulf Arab regimes have recently devoted themselves to the task of tailoring the regionally similar brand to reflect separate, distinctly national characteristics.

The brand privileges individuals and nations but also differentiates them. Internally, it distinguishes native citizens from the many foreigners populating their cities. Externally, it helps each new nation to stamp its distinctive mark on world politics. Chapters five, six, and seven consider how these various regimes market the brand through novel, little-understood uses of public space. They are evident in spectacular national museums and vernacular architecture, in public ceremonies, in neo-Bedouin language, and in dress. The brand is adapted into new versions of tribal sports. It is also used to revise undesirable elements from the past, such as the hardships of pearling. Citizens are balancing contradictory expectations, norms, and values: cosmopolitan openness versus tribal isolationism; postnational globalization versus national specificities. These are not dichotomous but convergent styles, practices, and expectations.

Chapter eight looks at women's reactions to the new societies growing up around them. Some experience loss, others empowerment. Better educated than the men, women have unprecedented opportunities. Contesting tribal expectations that they remain at home and out of sight, they are entering public space and the workforce in growing numbers. Although some Gulf women seem poised to become important players in their societies, they still face the daunting challenge of negotiating the tensions between new opportunities and old constraints. Some women writers symbolize their fears in images that evoke cold and freezing. In conclusion, I consider a new social development with men and women rebelling against their societies' expectations and performing queer identities.

In the swirl of radical social transformation, Gulf Arabs are projecting a distinctive national and cultural identity that is rooted and tribal but also modern and global. Arab Gulf states are buying up iconic real estate around the world that compels attention to their wealth, prestige, and power. Since the outbreak of the Arab uprisings in January 2011, the tribal modern brand has expanded its significance, with Qatar claiming the right to become peace broker in the region.

Contesting contemptuous accounts of Gulf citizens' superficiality, lack of substance, and backwardness, I suggest that the return of the tribal is shaping a new way to think of the modern in cultural terms. It also opens a new way to conceptualize past and present, while imagining a previously unimaginable future. The tribal modern brand holds apparently contradictory states in balance. In the productive tension between a millennial source of social stability and a globalizing process of instant transformations, the tribal becomes a modernizing force.

In coining the term the "tribal modern," I am not imagining an alternative, culturally specific modernity, and certainly not an incomplete modernity. An apparent oxymoron, the tribal modern makes sense of the epistemological, socio-economic, and political upheavals that have rocked the Arab Gulf for half a century and continue to shape it today. Situated at the nexus of the local, the national, and the transnational, the tribal modern is a contact zone that recalls the miracle Saudi writer Raja' 'Alim invokes "where the old world and the new are tight as two lovers" ('Alim 2007, 217). Although this phenomenon is not limited to the Arab Gulf, it is there that this chronotope is most clearly in evidence.

CHAPTER ONE

Uneasy Cosmopolitanism

"Where are you from?" I asked the attendant at one of the women's dorms at Education City in Doha. Having noted the Qatari accent and the `abaya*, I had assumed that this woman was one of the few Qataris working a lowly job.

"Iran."

"Were you born in Iran?"

"No. Here."

"And your parents?"

"Here."

"And your grandparents?"

Nodding, she smiled. It was like sharing an insider joke. She knew the name of the town she was supposedly from but she was not sure where exactly it was located except that it was somewhere across the Gulf in the South. Near Shiraz? Yes, yes, near Shiraz.

I felt myself in a time warp. This "Iranian" woman reminded me of my South Asian travel companions in the human cargo boat almost forty years earlier. Children of those who stayed would probably have had her experience and felt the same way, but with a major difference. Indians cannot pass like those Iranians who look Arab.

A MILLENNIAL CROSSROAD

Since the 1960s, Asian workers have poured into the Gulf countries. Some have settled and had children, but virtually none have become citizens. Regular remittances to families across the Indian Ocean connect them to a home where they dream to return. So important are these laborers to the home economy that they have changed the face of some Asian villages and towns. Novelist Amitav Ghosh describes a road in Mangalore lined with "large houses, some new, with sharp geometric lines and bright pastel colours that speak eloquently of their owners' affiliations with the Persian Gulf" (Ghosh 1994, 284). These Asian immigrants are the latest in a long line of travelers who have moved back and forth across the vast oceanic spaces separating the Gulf from the western coasts of the Indian subcontinent and the eastern coasts of the African continent. Today the paths between the nodes of the ancient Indian Ocean network are more traveled than ever.

Rivaling the Pharaohs in their antiquity, these networks go back to the Bronze Age and the Bahrain-based civilization of Dilmun (2450–1700 BCE). Dilmun linked the ancient cities of Hufuf and Qatif in the eastern region of the Arabian Peninsula and Bahrain. Source of a cosmopolitan ethos that characterized the Gulf long before the rise of Islam, Dilmun was called *Ard al-khulud*, or the Land of Eternity. Mesopotamians, like Gilgamesh, the legendary king of Sumerian Uruk, went there hoping to escape death.[1] Recent archaeological excavations have made clear how broad and deep were the Gulf trading networks that connected Babylonia, Oman, East Africa, and the Indian subcontinent four millennia ago.[2] "Indus Valley seals have turned up at Ur and other Mesopotamian sites. 'Persian Gulf' types of circular stamped rather than rolled seals, known from Dilmun, that appear at Lothal in Gujarat, India, and Faylahkah, as well as in Mesopotamia, are convincing corroboration of the long-distance sea trade."[3]

By the ninth century CE, Gulf trade networks had spread to Southeast and even East Asia: "The recent discovery of an Arab *dhow* off the coast of Belitung in Indonesia laden with some 60,000 pieces of gold, silver, precious cobalt and white ninth-century Tang ceramics confirms the existence of a busy maritime trade route between Baghdad and Xian, capital of Tang China. Ships filled with aromatic woods from Africa and fine textiles and goods from Abbasid Baghdad would leave Basra and pass through the Gulf" (Fromherz 2012, 43–44). Sailors leaving the Gulf in November, their dhows full of pearls and dates, would return months later laden with spices, rice, sugar, and wood, especially Indian teak for doors and windows and Zanzibar mangrove poles for ceilings. With the wood and spices they also brought back new ideas and technologies from distant ports in the Indian Ocean.

These trading voyages generated prolonged contact between people separated by sea but linked by commerce. Writing about Kuwait, Anh Nga Longva describes long-distance ties that were common in the region: "Even ordinary merchants and sailors sometimes maintained households in both Kuwait and the towns along the trade route. Basra, Karachi, Calicut, Sur, Aden, Lamu, Mombasa, and Zanzibar were the nodal points through which pre-oil Kuwaiti society connected with the other participants in the sea-trade network centered around the Indian Ocean" (Longva 1997, 21). These men, whether from Kuwait or other Gulf ports, led multiple lives often with multiple wives.

From the earliest times, war, natural disasters, pilgrimage, and trade have attracted travelers to the Gulf region. Statues in the trading hub of Thaj just west of Dammam provide evidence of a lesser-known stop along the route of Alexander the Great's fourth-century BCE military conquests. In Yemen, the repeated ruptures of the Ma`rib Dam until the sixth century CE drove Yemenis out of the area, and many chose to move to the Gulf. From the seventh century, Muslim proselytizing and pilgrimage networks utilized the ancient frankincense and spice caravan routes. Beginning in the sixteenth century, Indian Ocean and Mesopotamian subjects were trading and sparring with the Portuguese in the Gulf. More recently, imperial struggles between the Ottomans and the British brought new foreign elements into the mix. They fought for control of the valuable waterways that linked the Mediterranean with the Indian Ocean and the British with their Indian Raj.

By the second half of the nineteenth century, traffic in the Gulf had become intensely multicultural. Travelers, including pearl dealers from Paris, described a scene where Persians, Iraqis, Indians, Beluchis, Afghans, British, French, descendants of sixteenth-century Portuguese, Zanzibaris, Yemenis, Hadhramis, Palestinians, Syrians, and Lebanese all lived in the region (Al-Rasheed 2005, 3). In 1865, the British traveler William Palgrave described the colorful mix of foreigners in Manamah: "Thus the gay-coloured dress of the southern Persian, the saffron-stained vest of Oman, the white robe of Nejed, and the striped gown of Baghdad, are often to be seen mingling with the light garments of Bahreyn [...] Indians, merchants by profession, and mainly from Guzerat, Cutch, and their vicinity, keep up here all their peculiarities of costume and manner, and live among the motley crowd" (quoted in Onley 2005, 59).

When oil was discovered in the early twentieth century, a new group of migrants—Americans—entered the Gulf. Thus began the latest phase in Gulf cosmopolitanism.

CITIES OF SALT

For some, however, this period was less cosmopolitan than it was neocolonial. In the 1980s and early 1990s, several writers narrated the conversion of the desert into concrete jungles in a process as violent as the colonizing missions that the British and the French had brought to the Arab world in the nineteenth century. In his five-volume *Cities of Salt* (1989), Saudi oil economist and novelist in exile 'Abd al-Rahman Munif narrates the destructiveness of American oil imperialism that begins in the early 1930s in the fictional Wadi al-'Uyun, the Valley of Springs so named because of its many water springs.

The narrative unfolds a scene of betrayal. Generous as they might be to strangers who made it across the inhospitable territory that surrounded them, the tribes of the oasis kept to themselves. But one day it was rumored that three Franks, a.k.a. Christians, had arrived. Anxiety spread with the news that the foreigners spoke Arabic and they cited the Qur'an. Why had these strang-

ers come? Why were they asking so many questions "about dialects, about tribes, and their disputes, about religion and sects,
about the routes, the winds and the rainy seasons"? Why were
they so concerned to know whether other foreigners had pre-
ceded them (Munif 1989, 31)?

The Arabic-speaking foreigners were American oil prospectors who claimed to be looking for water. But the locals became
suspicious when the strangers' inquiries concerned remote
places not known to have wells or springs. The Americans stayed
a few days only to return several months later with many others,
and they set up camp. Alarmed, a local delegation confronted
the Emir, and he explained that he had invited the Americans
because they "have come to extract the oil and the gold" under
the tribes' feet; this oil and gold would make them all rich (86).
Soon, huge yellow machines filled the desert with their roar. By
the time they were done uprooting the palm trees and orchards
of the tribes, the invading Americans had reduced the idyllic
oasis to desert.

An agent of the local ruler plotting with the Americans warned
the people of Wadi al-'Uyun to leave if they wanted to be com-
pensated: "The emir has said good riddance to anyone who wants
their desert and tribe, but for those who want a *place* to live, the
government is arranging everything" (111, my emphasis). Wadi
al-'Uyun was thus not a real place, according to the American
understanding of place.

Everyone left, everyone, that is, except for a crazy old woman
who died the eve of the departure. The only way to stay in the
old Wadi al-'Uyun was to be buried in its sand. Now this newly
desertified space "that no longer had a name since the houses
had been destroyed and all the landmarks obliterated" (187) was

ready to be turned into the kind of place where camels, the *sine qua non* of pre-oil tribal life, no longer were of use. Without camels the tribes had no means of livelihood. To survive they had to work with the Americans.

Meanwhile, the Americans established themselves in Harran, a hellhole of a place on the Gulf. It was to be "a port and head-quarters of the company, as well as a city of finality and damnation ... Within less than a month two cities began to rise: Arab Harran and American Harran"[4] (198, 206). After American Harran had been built, the Arabs wanted their city to be just like it. But that was not to be.[5] Housed in barracks, the Bedouin were reduced to laborers who watched the Americans cavort and "do just as they please in their own *colony*" (216, my emphasis). In true colonial fashion, the Americans had asserted power over potential rebels.[6] The novel trumpets a warning: outsiders are dangerous; their desire for the Arabs' land and wealth must be checked.[7]

The Bedouin had treated the American oil prospectors with the suspicion they reserved for outsiders. Outsiders were not from Mars; they were part, albeit an unwanted part, of their lives, and the Bedouin had always kept them on the edge of their society. These latest outsiders, however, could not be prevented from venturing deep into Bedouin territory. Their desire for black gold would keep them there indefinitely.

CONTAMINATION

Munif's novel fictionalizes a process that became increasingly painful with the discovery and exploitation of oil throughout the Gulf region. As Harrans mushroomed all around the Gulf coasts, foreigners began to outnumber the native population. The stream of workers has grown exponentially and, with their exploding numbers, the fear factor. Even though most of the migrants are the poorest of the poor from Asia and Africa, utterly dependent on their local sponsors, without any rights and with the most meager of hopes to sustain families back home, their visibility everywhere has led to fear of their contaminating influence and a determination to deny them the rights and entitlements of citizenship.[8] Gulf regimes have instituted exclusionary policies that range from "formal categorization and legislation to informal customs and practices in everyday life and the manipulation of cultural values and symbols" (Longva 1997, 44). Some of these exclusions are institutionalized; others are symbolic. No matter how long they have lived there, the vast majority of foreigners remain physically and socially apart from the citizen community. Prevented from integrating, they must stay ever alert to internal borders they cannot cross.[9]

In their segregation, they become the "Other," a single block of alterity in whose mirror Gulf Arabs see their own identity reflected. But within this block, the international workers are socially stratified and enclosed in ethnic compounds. What sociologist Asef Bayat observes about Dubai might be said about any of the Gulf states: "Dubai turns out to be no more than a 'city-state of relatively gated communities' marked by sharp communal and spatial boundaries, with labor camps (of South Asian migrants) and the segregated milieu of parochial jet-setters, or the 'cosmopolitan' ghettos of the western elite expatriates who remain bounded within the physical safety and cultural purity of their own reclusive collectives" (Bayat 2010, 186–87; see also Khalaf 2006, 251–56). A chasm yawns between the native citizens and both sets of others: the educated cosmopolitans and the laboring underclass.

With no hope of acquiring citizenship[10] or of returning home because of the crushing debts they owe their sponsors, the migrant laborers survive in slums on the city margins or in desert camps. For second- and third-generation workers, to be Pakistani in Dubai does not designate a country of origin. It means belonging to a group of rootless people who live, work, and die together with compatriots in the only place they know to call home: Dubai, Abu Dhabi, Sharjah, Umm al-Quwain, Ajman, Fujairah, Qatar, Bahrain, and Kuwait. They have no rights. They are thrown together in what looks like the "everyday cosmopolitanism" of multicultural urban centers, but with a difference. For if cosmopolitanism is "both a social condition and an ethical project... with humanistic objectives," as Asef Bayat maintains, then what we see in the Gulf is not cosmopolitanism but communalism of the "inward-looking and close-knit ethnic or religious collectives [who] espouse narrow, exclusive, and selfish interests" (Bayat 2010, 186). There is good reason to place foreigners in enclaves. When a financial crisis occurs, projects are put on hold, and foreign laborers risk being dispatched so that life for the native citizens may continue generally undisturbed. Adam Hanieh uses the term "spatialization" to explain how such geo-political mechanisms of social control allow for the "spatial displacement of crisis" (Hanieh 2011, 60, 63, 65, 179).

Although Americans and Europeans are accorded privileges generally unavailable to South and Southeast Asians and to Africans, internal distinctions place the wealthy maharaja above the middle-class European. Wealth trumps ethnicity among the professional expatriates whom Longva calls "educated cosmopolitans." Making up the middle classes between the Gulf Arabs and the manual laborers, this "ethnically composite population shared one common feature, a 'creolized' expatriate culture with elements from multiple origins expressed in a major Western idiom—mostly English, occasionally French—and coalesced around values that were perceived as Western" (Longva 1997, 136). These educated cosmopolitans "close ranks across nationalities, united in their eager embracement of 'Western' identity" (138). In other words, a Westernized identity has become legible as middle-class status. Class notwithstanding, native citizens view most outsiders with a suspicion that may escalate to panic.

"Expatriates are a danger worse than the atomic bomb," some officials recently warned.[11] Under intense surveillance, they experience a discrimination common "in modern societies characterized by an advanced system of social welfare since, to be genuinely meaningful, these social goods are necessarily limited, and their enjoyment is therefore contingent on proof of national membership" (Longva 1997, 7; see Longva 2005, 126). This proof nowadays is visible and audible. It is performed in dress and language that distinguish the native citizens from the immigrant workers. The streets, where the non-citizens come into contact with the citizens and where "collective dissent may be both expressed and produced" (Bayat 2010, 167), attract the greatest scrutiny. Even if the non-citizens do not intend to rebel, their mere public presence drives the authorities to "normalizing violence, erecting walls and checkpoints, as a strategic element of everyday life . . . [for the disenfranchised] the streets are the main, perhaps the only place where they perform their daily functions—to assemble, make friends, earn a living, spend their leisure time, and express discontent. In addition, streets are also the public places where the state has the most evident presence, which is expressed in police patrol, traffic regulations, and spatial divisions" (12, 62, 212). Streets are systematically surveilled to make sure undesirables, especially working-class bachelors, stay out of sight and back in their desert camps.

During weekends and holidays, plain-clothes police instinctively sort the sheep from the goats of Asian flaneurs and shoo them away. To the uninitiated, the fine distinctions between social classes within a single national group disappear in the casual attire of public leisure places. Yet, the local police can smell class even across the six-lanes that some workers in their Sunday best are trying to cross in order to join the families enjoying the Corniche or public parks. In mufti and trying to act like everyone else, the plain-clothed police stride toward the spot their prey is approaching. Just as he recognizes them, so they recognize him. Most give up. For the hardy few, those who dare to assert civic rights of access to public places, there's a brief encounter. The courageous are humiliated and compelled to slink back. They had misread open space for a public place. They were guilty of violating public interest, interest that depends on keeping social classes separate (Chakrabarty 2002, 77).

The management of foreigners has produced two separate domains, the pure and the contaminated. Saudi Raja' ʿAlim explores these separate worlds in her Mecca novels that mix magic, perfume, and fantasy. Although strangers are the norm in a Mecca where pilgrims often stay and become part of the city's life, the Meccans keep them at a distance. Sri Lankans, Indonesians, and Ethiopians stave off hunger, she writes, by "eating vermin and drinking the water of Zamzam" (`Alim 2007, 158). These outsiders with their disgusting diets and broken Arabic bear the contamination of what they eat: vermin. The holy waters of the Zamzam well may counteract the dire consequences of their condition, yet they remain a source of dread (158, 162, 230, 236–37).

Post-oil mass migrations to the Arab Gulf have caused anxiety that verges on panic. Native citizens fear that the foreigners, who outnumber them everywhere except in Bahrain, will become what Asef Bayat calls a social non-movement. The power of such actors emerges out of their large numbers and their "*common* practices of *everyday life*" (Bayat 2010, 20, original emphasis). Poised to unite in what Hannah Arendt has called a tribal nationalism with no "definite home but (feeling) at home wherever other members of their 'tribe' happened to live" (Arendt 1979, 232), these rootless inside-outsiders threaten to demand a share in the national wealth. To deflect a potential rights discourse and maintain their monopoly over resources, Gulf Arabs emphasize their deep history in a region "free" of foreigners.[12] The narrative of a pure past is a fiction, but it is a fiction with strong roots in the psychological stress of the present moment when black gold is producing new contradictions.

FORGET THE MULTICULTURAL PAST

The region's rich multicultural history is being erased. This erasure appears most clearly in the surprising rewriting of merchant histories. The families of traders who have long connected crucial nodes in the Indian Ocean networks "downplay or deny their transnational heritage in response to the Arabization policies of the Gulf Arab governments [...] In the Gulf today, public discussion about the Persian, Indian, and African mothers of past shaikhs and shaikhas is strongly discouraged" (Onley 2005, 60, 62). Any discussion of such intermarriage in the past challenges the purity of twenty-first-century Gulf Arabs and so it is erased. Although "multiculturalism has defined the Gulf since time immemorial" (Fox, Mourtada-Sabbah, and al-Mutawa 2006, 267), it dissolves in myths of millennial isolation.

Yet, tribal elites' rejection of a past filled with cross-cultural encounters is not anomalous. Rather, it mirrors a reflex of modernity that promotes "the systematic erasure of continuous and deep-felt encounters [that] have marked human history throughout the globe" (Trouillot 2002, 846). "Spectacular domination's first priority," Guy Debord confirms, "was to eradicate historical knowledge in general; beginning with just about all rational information and commentary on the most recent past…The more important something is, the more it is hidden…Spectacular power can deny whatever it likes, once, or three times over, and change the subject, knowing full well there is no danger of any riposte, in its own space or any other" (Debord 1998, 13–14, 19). On the palimpsest of the now empty page, tribal leaders and their historians can pen new stories of spotless lineages.

What has changed in contemporary Gulf countries is not the fact of multiculturalism, but rather its agents and its scale: "Iranians and Indians still live in the Gulf Arab ports, but few Gulf Arabs have connections with Iran or India today. The predominant foreign influence is now British and American" (Onley 2005, 78). The new cosmopolitan story accents a past of uncontaminated lineages and isolated lifestyles. The less said about that heterogeneous past the better; the fantasy of first exposure to outsiders must be maintained.

Wealth and anxiety about who should have it and who should not even dream of wanting it have combined to create a climate of cruel discrimination against the foreign majority, especially the Asian laborers. But there are some, like Qatari poet Maryam Ahmad Al Subaiey, who acknowledge the humanity and suffering of people whose labor has turned the desert into a paradise for the few:

> Behind the dust all you can see
> is their broken souls and the shine
> of new cars mirrored in their eyes.
> They are not as human as we are.
> They are nothing
> but workers. We don't want
> them in our malls, we choose
> not to see them, to forget them.
> This army that builds our country
> remains invisible beneath the burning sun.
>
> Paine, Lodge, and Touati 2011, 171–72

Al Subaiey rails at her fellow citizens' collective indifference that has reduced these foreigners to the broken life of the barely human. Beneath the burning sun, the invisible army builds a brave new world for the native citizens, the privileged minority. It is their rights as tribal citizens that the police monitor and safeguard.

Chapter two will consider the ways in which Gulf Arabs project tribal modern identities that accord them rights and privileges unavailable to those without their pure tribal blood. New DNA testing bolsters oral histories of millennial tribal endogamy and the family trees they generate. This kind of tribal lineage determines citizenship and concomitant entitlements to a share in the oil wealth.

Pure Blood and the New Nation

Tribalism that considers every outsider, even a
neighbor, a permanent foreigner

Bagader, Heinrichsdorff, and Akers 1998

It could be argued that the tribal 'tradition,' especially
in relation to the marriage practices of women,
traditional dress and expected social roles is often
increased, not decreased by wealth and the pursuit of
acceptable social status within an extremely wealthy
but still extremely lineage-based society

Fromherz 2012

In the fourteenth century, the Arab historian-philosopher Ibn
Khaldun (1332–1406) proposed a new way to think about the rise
and fall of civilizations. Humanity, he wrote, was divided between
two distinct forms of social organization or civilization, *badawa*
and *hadara*. *Badawa* is the space of the pastoral nomad Bedouin
forced by their circumstances to remain close to each other and
loyal to the tribe to survive. *Hadara*, by contrast, is the settled

place of urban ease where the blood bonds of tribal solidarity weaken and gradually come undone. Both are necessary to the ebb and flow of civilizations, and environment provides the key to understanding civilizational cycles as they oscillate in constant motion between these two extremes.

To my surprise, I learned that Ibn Khaldun's paradigm—at once dialectical and cyclical—still figures importantly in the way Gulf Arabs define themselves and their lineages. They know themselves to be *hadar* if their tribes had at some point in time settled in an oasis or on the coast, or *badawi* (Bedouin) if their tribes remained pastoral nomads. There is a psychological barrier between the two forms of tribal existence. One might even say that there is mutual contempt between these two tribal entities. The Bedouin consider the settled tribes "less honorable because they engaged in commerce rather than the noble pastime of camel raising. The *hadar* in turn saw themselves as more sophisticated than the nomads" (Rugh 2007, 17). In fact, *hadar* tends to trump Bedouin in a modern society that values the urban over the nomadic. But what is too easily lost in weighing whether *hadar* or Bedouin prevail is the persistence of their interaction. These native citizens of rapidly transforming city-states lining the eastern shore of the Arabian Peninsula are both modern and tribal.

During spring 2008, I visited a class in Georgetown-Qatar University, one of the new American branch campuses housed in Doha's Education City. I asked the students whether the concept of the tribal modern meant anything to them. The unanimous response: "Of course! Tribal roots is everyone's new thing!" They explained that when meeting each other for the first time, they would try to discover each other's tribes by asking "Aish ismitch" (or, "What is your name?"—that is, what's the name of your tribe?). Some students were even more direct: "To which tribe do you belong?" Was there a contradiction in their minds, I asked, between being modern while also asserting the importance of tribal affiliations? No, they replied, the tribal is cool. But, they quickly added, it's not enough to be from a tribe, any tribe; what mattered was which tribe. The tribe had to be elite, with an impressive lineage, for it to be really cool.

Elsewhere, in a filmed exchange among Qatari students, one boy claimed that all Qataris were originally Bedouin. His friends remonstrated, calling Bedouin backward. The coup de grace came when one of them sneered: "Just look at their cars!" To which the we-are-all-Bedouin boy responded, "No, you can't tell the Bedouin by their cars. Now they have nice cars. You can only tell who are the real Bedouin from their language."[1] In chapter seven, I discuss why the revival of the Bedouin language has become so popular among young people in the region.

Before oil, Arab Gulf tribes with their clans lived in their own defined and bounded territory. Their territories stretched across what later became national borders. The tribe's right to be there, like the shaikh's right to assert hegemony, was based on a historical claim. It was a claim undergirded by power and genealogies. Rivalries, alliances, political marriages, and colonial interventions all choreographed the intricate dance of power that allowed individual tribal leaders to hold on to their territory during the early oil period while also becoming rulers of new nation-states.[2]

THE BRITISH

The British arrived in the Gulf in the late eighteenth century. It was a turbulent period, with tribal leaders feuding and pirates roaming the coasts. Abdulaziz Al Mahmud has captured the spirit of the age in *The Corsair.* The novel narrates the bitter conflict between clueless British emissaries and the notorious Rahmah ibn Jabir Al Jalahimah. Considered a folk hero for his resistance to the British in the early nineteenth century, Kuwait's Barbarossa made and broke alliances with the various rulers in the region, thus often outwitting the British.

Already well established in India, however, the British were able to exert increasing control, and, in 1820, they signed the General Treaty of Peace with the shaikhs of the Oman coast and Bahrain. The treaty banned pirate attacks on their ships and at the same time outlawed maritime toll collection in the Gulf. The 1853 Maritime Truce renewed various earlier treaties aimed at controlling piracy, barring foreign powers from playing a role in the region, and keeping shipping lanes open (Davidson 2008, 19; Bristol-Rhys 2011, 45). The British policy of mediating tribal rivalries and ending piracy was less altruistic than it was strategic, because before the opening of the Suez Canal in 1869, the Gulf was the main thoroughfare from England to India. British colonials and their East India Company ships needed safe passage from the English Channel to the Indian Ocean.

The treaties signed with the British empowered and legitimized the ruling shaikhs. They also brought the small shaikhdoms into the "international state system as autonomous political entities" (Crystal 1990, 17).[3] The shaikhdoms became part of the British Commonwealth, where all subjects were vouchsafed imperial protection. In the Gulf, not only Arabs but also Indian traders, who enjoyed a virtual monopoly over the pearling industry until the late nineteenth century, were British Commonwealth subjects.

The British made sure that the Indians were not harassed (Lorimer 1984, 808–11).

By the end of the nineteenth century, British power in the Gulf region expanded, thanks to their systematic data collection, the sine qua non for organization and control of their colonies. They were the first to record the existence of the shaikhdoms and to recognize them as distinct political entities. In so doing, they conferred external recognition and power on ruling families who "could trace their origins back to one of the Arabian Peninsula tribes. With their rule sanctioned and supported by the British, the ruler drew wealth from taxes on pearling, trade, as well as some agricultural activities" (Hanieh 2011, 5). It was a huge shift in both perception and power. The British insisted on a pure tribal lineage to qualify someone to negotiate, and their insistence on designating and prioritizing some tribes over others became crucial ultimately, not only to defining citizenship but also to assigning economic and political rights.

In 1899, John Gordon Lorimer, official of the Indian Civil Service, put together *The Gazetteer of the Persian Gulf, Oman and Central Arabia.* According to the title, the Gulf coast was considered one region, the desert hinterland another, with Oman the only named country. Lorimer, working under Vice-Regent Lord Curzon, employed a team of researchers from the Political Department of the British Government in India. During eight long years, *The Gazetteer* researchers collected information on local tribes. Above all, they noted when the various states were first mentioned by their current name. For example, the little fishing village where the Bani ʿUtub of the Central Arabian tribe of ʿUnaiza settled in 1716 was called Kut, or Kuwait. In 1766, immigrants from Kuwait moved to "Zubarah, upon the western shore of the promontory of Qatar" (Lorimer 1984, 787). At the time, Qatar was a dependency of Bahrain (798).

The Gazetteer became an instrument of rule, an invaluable manual and a symbolic register of prestige for Gulf Arabs and also for the British. It gave the British an idea of tribes' material wealth and relative usefulness to the British. Unlike other British colonies rich in natural resources or history, the Gulf shaikhdoms were considered a nuisance factor to be minimized in order for business-as-usual to proceed throughout the British Empire. Although they did wield political influence in the region, the British had little presence on land. They preferred to use local agents to conduct their business (Bristol-Rhys 2011, 50).

Far from resisting what might have been considered to be a colonizing project, Bahrain in 1861 asked the British to admit them to what came to be called the Truce. Other shaikhdoms followed suit. So positive was the British presence considered to be that when the British government "declared it could no longer afford the 12,000,000 pounds per annum to keep its forces in the Gulf and would be withdrawing its military in 1971, the Ruler of Abu Dhabi offered to pay for the military presence himself. The Ruler of Dubai made a similar offer . . . The British Government declined these unprecedented offers, however, and withdrew its forces in December 1971" (Onley and Khalaf 2006, 192, 202, 203, 204). When one considers the nature of colonial rule and its end in other parts of Asia and in Africa, this scenario is nothing short of extraordinary. Although 1971 is now said to be the date of independence for all Gulf countries except for Kuwait, which had declared independence in the early 1960s, it was not marked by revolt or warfare but rather by reluctance. Only when offers to sponsor Britain's continued military presence failed did the shaikhdoms organize themselves into separate nation-states. The UAE formed a new confederation from the Council of the Trucial States that had been established in 1952.

New national boundaries in effect "froze tribal relationships at the point the maps were finalized and further removed the rationale for many past tests of leadership" (Rugh 2007, 13).[4] Borders hardened as lines drawn through tribal territories during the early oil period came to account for nationally distinct characteristics.

Nationalism did not erase tribalism so much as shift its focus. Nationalizing tribal identities while still insisting on their importance, modern regimes held tribal lineage in affective tension with the national identity. Just as Ibn Khaldun could not conceive of civilization apart from the dynamic of Bedouin and urban theaters, so the modern Gulf states are unimaginable apart from the tribal and national spheres of identity. Beyond language, culture and, crucially, tribal blood, what were the unique characteristics of national belonging in these territorially small but economically potent countries that had been formed at the same time and shared the same history? That is the question that I explore in the following pages.

NATIONALIZING TRIBES

There is nothing natural or unchanging about blood lineages. As in all cases of modern state and nation formation, blood ties only seem to "naturally bind its members together while 'naturally' separating races and nations [and naturalizing] obligations and responsibilities towards race and nation, and not towards outsiders" (Thobani 2007, 113). In other words, what is not natural is made to appear as natural. This racialization process homogenizes heterogeneous populations. Race, David Goldberg writes, "is integral to the emergence, development and transformations (conceptually, philosophically, materially) of the modern nation-state" (quoted in Thobani 2007, 24). Tribe becomes race becomes nation, but each step depends on practices of ranking, imposition, and control to sustain the links and secure power for those privileged by such links.

In the Arab Gulf, racialized nation building confronted a local problem. National borders often cut through tribal territories, and tribal affiliations split when individual members had to choose different nationalities with their rights and entitlements to vote, to buy property, and to marry. The same tribe then provided the same qualification for national citizenship but in two states. The tribal system, Amira Sonbol argues, has suffered.[5] This is true, but it is also true that tribes could and did find new ways of dealing with tribal ambiguity so that demands for national homogeneity should not undermine tribal identity.

Not all tribes saw the advantage in choosing a single citizenship, preferring the freedom of pastoral nomadism. Some of those who did not register for citizenship remain even today without the rights and entitlements of those who did choose to belong to one of the new nation-states. This "withoutness" earned them the name Bedoon, meaning "without." It is important to recognize that this statistically small group represents the residue of a larger, often inchoate process of choice that all Gulf Arabs faced with nationalization. Recently, the Bedoon have become assertive. While the Bedoon did not choose any nationality, other tribes, like the Al Murrah,[6] did choose several nationalities precisely because they continued to privilege tribal boundaries over national borders. Used to wandering freely across lands where they had established control "through military conquest and displacement of other tribes" (Cole 1975, 94), members of the Al Murrah in 2005 refused to recognize the Qatar–Saudi Arabia border that had once again been recognized by a treaty protocol in 2001.[7] Consequently, those Al Murrah who did not choose exclusive Qatari citizenship were forced to leave when the government cut off their water and electricity. In May 2005, "members of the Al Ghafran clan, a division of the Murrah tribal confederation, wrote to US congressmen to complain that they'd been stripped of their Qatari citizenship" (O'Sullivan 2008, 21, 220; see Al-Qassemi 2012). Why U.S. congressmen? Probably because of the close relationship established between the Qatari and the American governments after 9/11. The presence of the United States Central Command, or CENTCOM, just outside Doha city limits, means that Americans have influence and power. In effect, the U.S. was assuming the oversight role that the British had previously exercised. The Qatari government did soon restore the Al Murrah their citizenship, but not before the lingering potential for ongoing tension between tribal and national had been registered yet again.

Like all Gulf Arab tribes, the Al Murrah had to choose between nationalities while continuing to assert the purity of their tribal lineage. Purity and authenticity, or *asala*, was the *sine qua non* for national citizenship. The overlapping and confusion of tribal and national identities are part of everyday life. Noof al-Khalifa illustrates the dilemma through a story about her Bahraini great-great-grandfather, Shaikh Nasser bin Mubarak bin Abdullah, who married the daughter of the Qatari Shaikh Jassim bin Mohammad Al Thani, and now she wonders, "Where do I belong? I know I'm a *Muslim*, an *Arab*, and a *Qatari*. I come from a big family, the Al Khalifas, with complicated roots [that stretch back to Bahrain]" (Al Khalifa 2010, 42). By downgrading the tribal affiliation, Noof could acquire the modern religious, ethnic and, above all, national identity that made her a Qatari citizen.

TRIBAL MODERN MARRIAGES

"From the time of Adam," says Dabbasi, a Bedouin in Munif's *Cities of Salt*, "men have bound themselves together by way of women. When a man gets married he binds himself to the land and the tribe" (Munif 1989, 261). Tribal marriages depend, above all, on women who uphold the purity of the lineage by not marrying down. These marriages remain crucial in societies where tribal affiliation constitutes qualification for citizenship.

Yet tribal marriages are complicated because they take place within the limits of nation and often "tribal equivalence." These protocols have serious consequences for women. Should they wish to marry a foreigner, native citizens may have to seek official permission, and, if denied, women may have to give up their citizenship, because children automatically inherit their father's citizenship and its rights. In 1989, the state of Qatar passed a law, Qatari Law No. 21, which "banned certain categories of state employees from marrying foreigners at all: ministers and deputy ministers, members of the diplomatic service, officers of the armed forces, the police or intelligence service, and students on overseas study-missions" (Dresch 2005, 149). Far from being exceptional, the Qatari Law has its equivalents elsewhere in the Gulf (155).[8]

But none of the laws answer fully the larger question: who counts as foreign when the tribal and the national are confused? A foreigner might be a first cousin. For example, should the citizen of one state wish to marry his daughter to the son of a brother who had chosen another nationality, he will face a dilemma, since this nephew now counts as a foreigner. In an April 1999 colloquium in Ras al-Khaima on marriage to foreign women, some women participants demanded clarification for the definition of foreigner (Dresch 2005, 152). No clear answer emerged beyond a reversion to DNA as biological (i.e., tribal) proof of nationality. Conference organizers declared that the Emiratis' distinguishing feature is "relationships of kinship and descent (*al-qurba wa-l-nasab*) among families within the state. This again harks back to the criterion of purity or authenticity. It connects tribal membership and citizenship rights to authentic (*asli*, original, noble) Arab customs and manners which originate from the (the society's) Islamic belief and from ethical values inherited from (our) ancestors" (155). In fact, it is kinship and descent among families within the state that provide the biological definition, and the nod to Islam reinforces the ethical dimension. Since the notion of citizenship in the Arab Gulf is a recent invention, this insistence on nationals marrying each other can, and often does, undermine endogamous tribal bonds spanning the Arabian Peninsula.

The question of who can marry whom assumes added significance for rulers and their families. In her study of the political culture of leadership in the UAE, Andrea Rugh emphasizes the importance of tribal marriages in strengthening the status of the leader and his tribe: marriages consolidate blood ties, reward loyalty, and sometimes co-opt enemies (Rugh 2007, 82–95, 137, 191, 227).

Since the early 1990s, some governments have established a *sunduq al-zawaj* (marriage fund) that offers monetary inducements to marry within the nation-state. The UAE, for example, provides a 20,000-Dirham dowry, substantial funds for national weddings, and subsidies for children (Fox, Mourtada-Sabbah, and al-Mutawa 2006, 47; see also Bristol-Rhys 2011, 88; Longva 1997, 53). The marriage fund also underwrites the costs of mass weddings. In March 2000, 376 Dubai couples "were married off at once in an enormous televised ceremony, where questions of status among families were displaced by eulogies to Dubai's crown prince and to the Federation's leader, Shaikh Zayed of Abu Dhabi [...] The Fund represents a massive attempt at social engineering" (Dresch 2005, 148; see Hasso 2011, 72). In this case, nation trumped tribe and tribal equivalence. What mattered was the fact that citizens of the same nation-state were strengthening the national composition of the state and that, in the future, their children would swell the citizen roles.[9] Tribal equivalence and compatibility, however, remain factors in deciding marriage partners.

When I asked some Qatari students about tribal equivalence and how to tell who is where in the tribal pecking order, they said that everyone knows.

"But *how* do you know?" I asked.

They shrugged, smiling at the strangeness of the question: "You can tell from the face to which tribe this person belongs. You can tell their status by the way they speak or act or dress."

"Why does tribal status matter so much?"

"If you marry someone from an inappropriate tribe, you harm the tribe."

What did harming the tribe mean? To look more deeply into the affective connection between tribal class and marriage, I asked several students in a class I was teaching at the Virginia Commonwealth University–Qatar (VCUQ) in the fall of 2010 to conduct surveys on the role of tribal class and on the importance of *asala* (or, authenticity and purity of lineage) in marriage.

Thirty men and women between the ages of 18 and 30 responded in full to an online survey about tribal status and the acceptability of marriage outside the tribe.[10] One of the questions that the students had left optional was tribal name. To the students' surprise, most of the respondents were happy to give the name of their tribe. Moreover, some even specified whether they were *hadar* or Bedouin.

A majority of respondents affirmed that elite tribe members should marry each other. One simply wrote: "Of course!" Another: "Yes, because our society is extremely tribal." For another, the tribes are the "good *pure* part of society" (emphasis in the original).

In answer to a question about what makes a tribe elite, several insisted on the importance of deep roots in time and across space. A member of the Al Muraikhi tribe, for instance, wrote that her Bedouin tribe stretched in space to "KSA (Kingdom of Saudi Arabia), Kuwait, Qatar and UAE...some are in Bahrain too. We go back before Islam, i.e. more than 1400 years ago!" In other words, she perceived her status to derive from the geographic and temporal spread of her tribe. A man from the Al Suba`i tribe wrote that he could trace ancestors for over 1000 years; members of his tribe can be found "almost in all Arab countries." An Al Murrah man also affirmed pride in his tribe. Careful not to seem arrogant, he added, "If my tribal habits is [*sic*] making others embarrassed I don't show them or present it. Being around people who don't belong to tribes, trying not to make them feel they lack something." His self-evident tribal superiority, he presumed, would embarrass and even intimidate anyone without elite tribal affiliation. "I am *asil* Arab from the Arabian Gulf," wrote one woman, using the Arabic term *asil* in her otherwise English statement.

Although the expectation to marry within tribal equivalence is widespread, the student survey probed personal feelings on the subject: would they accept a spouse from another tribal class? 70.6 percent said yes. One wrote, "I would choose to marry a person based on compatibility, respect, love, mutual understanding, etc. [*sic*] and not only based on their tribal origin or their last name!" Note that none of these affective criteria trump tribal origin. Instead, they become additive, desirable traits.

While they were not the majority, a third of the responses indicated that the partner's tribal status, class, did indeed matter to them. The following is a sampling of these reactions:

"Lower social class affects my kids."

"I do not accept other tribes and their customs."

"When it comes to marriage it is very hard and rare to break the rules; basically we just can't."

"It is impossible for me to marry someone from another tribal class."

How absolute this person was! Even political status cannot overcome lack of tribal equivalence.[11]

"The tribe must have *hasab* (noble descent) and *nasab* (tribal lineage)" (Khaldunian terms were here used seamlessly, almost reflexively, to denote status and kinship categories).

"Maybe I won't be able to interact with other tribes and my family might not accept that."

The most amusing reply came from a woman who listed the eight appropriate tribes for herself and for her children, ending with a flourish: "Can you mix diamonds with stainless steel? Doesn't work."

Some wrote that they would impose the same tribal restrictions on their children, indicating their satisfaction with a system that should be perpetuated. Although two-thirds of the participants in the survey had responded that tribal class in a life partner did not matter to them individually, the overwhelming majority agreed that their families did care. One wrote that to marry someone with Persian blood is completely unacceptable. In the summary of the survey results, the students wrote that they were surprised to learn that these marriage restrictions were not imposed: "They actually believe in them to a degree that they want to apply these tribal restrictions on their children."

The principle of tribal compatibility in marriage, or *kafa'a*, has long governed tribal alliances.[12] Whereas men may marry down, women should not. Women's hypogamy degrades her tribe's gene pool because children carry the father's tribal affiliation. Although *kafa'a* is an Islamic legal principle ruling on the suitability of marriage partners, `*adam takafu' al-nasab* is a deviation from that principle. In Sunni schools of jurisprudence, *kafa'a* rules on compatibility between a man and a woman amount to "equivalence of social status, fortune and profession (those followed by the husband and by the father-in-law), as well as parity of birth, which should exist between husband and wife, in default of which the marriage is considered ill-matched and, in consequence, liable to break-up."[13] In the Gulf, lack of tribal lineage compatibility (`adam takafu' al-nasab`) can sometimes entail what some call "forced divorce." In this latest usage, `adam takafu' al-nasab` accentuates the importance of *nasab* or tribal lineage. Authorities can force a couple to divorce or not to marry if their tribes are unequal. Despite concern about skyrocketing divorce rates in the region,[14] police even have permission to pursue a tribally incompatible couple and force them to divorce. Saudi poet Nimah Nawwab decries this practice and the continued dominance of tribal values. She wonders why "this abhorrent tribalistic attitude and practice has again resurged after its eradication by Islam."[15]

DNA AND MONEY

Yet, money and the class mobility it enables complicate tribal equivalence. How can hypergamy for women be sustained in the oil age when members of lower tribes become superrich and thus change their class, and with it, their tribal status? Blood and bank accounts compete.

A young Emirati woman complained that her grandmother would prefer her to marry a foreigner rather than a man from a lower status tribe: " 'No way in the world would she let that happen, because they used to work for us; in her eyes that would be like marrying the driver, for God's sake.' When I point out that the family in question is fabulously wealthy and well-respected now, I get a look that tells me that I am incredibly dense" (Bristol-Rhys 2011, 99). The tone of outrage at the mere thought of marrying down, even if to super-rich men, mirrors some of the responses to the VCUQ tribal marriage surveys: "Tribal class is more important than money in my family. Money goes but family name will stay." Another wrote: "Being rich is not what I ask from the man. We all have money." Time will tell how long such indifference to money can last.

Incalculable wealth, how it is to be distributed, and who has the right to what size of the pie, is changing attitudes. It has given tribal compatibility a new twist. One principle pervades: money should not seep out of the hands of the pure tribes. For anthropologists John and Jean Comaroff, "the more that ethnically defined populations move toward the model of the profit-sharing corporation, the more their terms of membership tend to become an object of concern, regulation, and contestation. And the more they do, the greater is their proclivity to privilege biology and birthright, genetics and consanguinity, over social and cultural criteria of belonging" (Comaroff and Comaroff 2009, 47, 65). Blood and money can, and sometimes do, replace the flexible forms of social community that used to prevail: "nowhere was there full agreement as to family or collective history. Though ambiguity has not disappeared, the arbiter is now a state apparatus, which rules upon genetic facts" (Dresch 2006, 203). No longer part of a flexible oral tradition, lineage is now being fixed, and the state is ruling upon genetic facts.[16]

Tribal concerns with pure blood in the Gulf parallel developments in South Africa, with new demands to draw "unequivocal lines of inclusion and exclusion, of inside and out. No wonder the commerce in recreational genomics, which turns out to be more than merely recreational when the stakes are large, is growing so quickly; the likes of DNA PRINT GENOMICS, DNA Tribes, and Ethnoancestors claim to have technologies that provide 'hard' scientific evidence of identity, evidence that puts the matter of membership beyond construction, debate, or question" (Comaroff and Comaroff 2009, 67).[17]

Scientific evidence silences pesky questions not only about who is a pure Gulf Arab, but strangely also about who is a pure Emirati, pure Bahraini, pure Qatari, or pure Kuwaiti. In Kuwait, "DNA samples might be taken to see who is and who is not Kuwaiti ... what was previously judged by diffuse public opinion is now judged by state bureaucracy" (Dresch 2006, 203). In Doha, the Shafallah Medical Genetics Center investigates genetic diseases it believes are caused by intermarriage—autism, diabetes and Down syndrome—and the wonders of pure Qatari blood. Leading a small group of visitors through the facilities and to the genetic research center in December 2008, the director spoke about the greater concentration of genes in the Qatari population caused by consanguinity. Thirty percent of marriages take place between first cousins in what he called an "isolate society." While the prevalence of hereditary disease is a major problem, he said, it is also proof of the purity of Qatari bloodlines. *Qatari* blood, not *tribal* blood, is paraded as the true criterion of authenticity. He was talking about raced national citizens. This is a remarkable, if not singular, instance of government involvement in the promotion of racial purity and superiority.

Recently, individual tribes have been constructing web pages that publicize their achievements, pedigree, and contribution to the success of the new nation-states. They are using social networking sites to stake a claim in the building of the nation-state that, in their view, has been overly identified with the ruling tribes who are distributing their own lineage maps linking them to the founder of their tribe.

CONCLUSION

Blood, as the basis of a clearly identified tribal identity, needs deep roots, and these roots then entwine with a deep, local, national history. The Kuwait government goes back to its first habitation on Failakha Island in the third millennium BCE. At the Bahrain Citadel, built by the Portuguese but said to be the capital of ancient Dilmun, museum visitors walk through layers of civilization from 2450 BCE, when Dilmun was a node in the Indus Valley–Babylonia trading network, to the Portuguese conquest in the sixteenth century. The Dubai museum of the Heritage Village boasts a 5000-year history uncovered in al-Sufuh, al-Qusais, and the British colony of Jumeirah. A poster in the museum celebrates Dubai's role "in establishing human civilization in the Gulf" (cited in Khalaf 2002, 34). The Msheireb museum on Doha's Corniche traces human habitation in Qatar back to the Stone Age. On National Day, December 17, 2008, Qatar's distinctive role in the early days of Islam was touted: "It is said the Prophet wore a Qatari robe, as did his wife Aisha" (*Qatar Peninsula*, December 17, 2008; see also O'Sullivan 2008, 211). Or was it just an Arabian robe?

Having established civilizational roots that antedate Europe's in Greece and Rome, state historians now work to piece together a national past that fragments the tribal networks that had connected all parts of the Arabian Peninsula. They then fit the tribal pieces within the circumference of the modern nation-state.

Blood becomes the core of a citizens' rights discourse that enshrines tribal origins.

But what is this tribal? Has it ever been only kinship arrangements and blood ties? Or, is it rather a social system and an *idea* providing symbolic capital for identity construction in societies where a dizzying rate of change renders life precarious? In the following chapter I will attempt to answer these questions.

CHAPTER THREE

The Idea of the Tribe

The *'idea' of the tribe* had to be preserved and even
enforced by the state, because its structure, being
based on a collective will, serves naturally as an
effective mechanism of control.   Arebi 1994

Tribalism in modern Arabia is alive and well.
Al-Qassemi 2012

In the 1960s and 1970s, rulers disaggregated tribal networks, settled many nomads, and invented new forms of affiliation more
acceptable and legible in the construction of modern nation-states.
Crucially, the name of the tribe was replaced by the tripartite
name, the *ism thulathi*, which recognized three generations only.
Tribal lineage beyond the grandfather was suppressed in order
to eradicate forms of sociality that seemed out of date and in conflict with the creation of modern national identities. That, at least,
was the official policy.

In the meantime, the region has witnessed transformations
never before imaginable outside the tales of the *Arabian Nights*.
Yet, so much from the tribal past persists, especially the norms

of leadership. Shaikhs had controlled their tribes and shaikhdoms through a complex system of reciprocal need and interdependence among foreigners, tribes, and merchant elites: "the core of the state apparatus (e.g. ministerial portfolios) went to members of the ruling family, while the concentric circles surrounding this core went to prominent merchant families and tribal allies of the ruler (e.g. positions in 'consultative assemblies') and other high-ranking state bodies" (Hanieh 2011, 66–68). The merchants, in particular, held power with the ruler because he depended on their political allegiance and the income they generated.

Rulers cultivated tribal loyalty through charisma and distribution of justice. They could not afford to alienate tribes, because when tribes shifted allegiance they took their tribal territory. In 1833, for example, Dubai declared its dissatisfaction with, and consequently its independence from, Abu Dhabi (Onley and Khalaf 2006, 196). Unjust rulers would lose their merchants and their pearl divers, the foundation of the local economy, when they protested unfair treatment and decided to migrate to a neighboring shaikhdom (197, see also Crystal 1990, 4–5). Although post-oil state formation and huge oil wealth have largely eliminated the arbitrariness of a system that had relied on tribes' and merchants' satisfaction with their stake in the system, what persist are the "commonly recognized obligations of rulership" that include eloquence, courage, generosity, and accessibility (Onley and Khalaf 2006, 198–99). Tribal ideals barely survive in evanescent notions of "egalitarianism, representation, consensus, accommodation, long genealogies, disdain for commerce" (Rugh 2007, 235–37). On the one hand, rulers increasingly distanced themselves from their people—they no longer opened their palaces to any and all subjects who wish to meet with them—and the new patronage state system promote relative anonymity. On the other hand, tribal-national leaders had the financial wherewithal to make native citizens feel content with their lot. Some saw in contemporary wealth distribution an extension of tribal politics in the guise of a hereditary welfare state where legitimacy "continues to be based on the sanctity of customs and 'traditions'... Rulership remains highly personalized" (Onley and Khalaf, 2006, 191, 205).

Within this dynamic context, the idea of the tribe has not only survived, it has become even more salient than before. New populations[1] and sources of wealth have centralized political and economic power in the hands of tribal rulers and their elites (Khoury and Kostiner 1990, 11). What before had been precariously managed now can be controlled, because fabulous wealth has freed rulers from their dependence on others (Rugh 2007, 13). The ruler's family and the inner circle of merchants continue to accumulate wealth. The merchants, however, have lost their discretionary power ceding it to the ruler's tribe members, especially to his immediate family.

Oil revenues "preserved continuity at the apex of the political system only by forcing the breakdown of the old ruling coalition and catalyzing the formation of a new pattern of political control" (Crystal 1990, 1). Rapid urban development has introduced numerous multinational corporations into the region and it is on them that rulers now depend (7). These corporations are now acquiring the kind of power and stake in the system that merchants had previously held. Oil undermined ruling coalitions, formed new systems of political control, and ushered in extra-territorial multinationals. It also created a new political subject: the national citizen.

Fuelling policies of radical exclusions, tribal hierarchies, and centralizing power, the idea of the tribe provides the cultural capital that undergirds twenty-first-century heritage engineering projects, none more spectacular than the return of the tribe as a port of refuge in a sea of foreigners.

INVENTION OF TRIBES

On the second of December 2010, Qatar won the FIFA (Federation Internationale de Football Association) bid for the 2022 World Cup. Promising to build nine state-of-the-art stadiums to be shipped after the games to countries unable to afford their own, Qatar had situated itself in the top tier of the sporting world by winning the right to host the world's most popular sport during its most important event (Fromherz 2012, 22).

The capital burst into two days of celebrations. By the third of December, the Corniche, which rings the bay, had turned into a parking lot with people sitting on top of their flag-draped, honking cars. At four o'clock, we saw a procession of camels making its way through the cars on the Corniche.

The riders in tribal costume were Dukhan Camel Club members. They had set out at five in the morning to make the eleven-hour trip to the capital in order to welcome the bidding team upon their return from Zurich. They wanted their Emir to know that he had made his people, his tribal people, proud to be part of his nation.

Such spectacular acknowledgments of a national tribal leader's achievement bring together otherwise divided national tribes. They are both *hadar* and Bedouin, and their cohesion ensures the success of the nation-state project. Educated and cosmopolitan,

Figure 2. Dukhan Camel Club welcomes the 2022 FIFA bidding team against the background of the Doha Bay skyscrapers.

the modern *hadar* contrast with the Bedouin tribes. The former drive SUVs and Lamborghinis; while the latter, like these members of the Dukhan Camel Club, ride dromedaries. Proudly, these modern Bedouin pitch their tents along the sides of highways on national and Islamic feast days. They perform folkloric dances (especially the `*arda* sword or battle dance, called `*ayyala* in the UAE) and make music. Such rituals, writes Thobani, "lie at the heart of social life, sustaining social bonds among members of the community through their repeated performance... sites where members of the collective perform their own belonging and recognize that of their compatriots... [they] promote the emerging racial hierarchy and enhance their access to politi-

Figure 3. "'*Arda* of the Al Bukawara shines during *Id al-Adha* (Feast of Sacrifice)"—headline in *Al-Raya*, November 16, 2010.

cal and economic power through the disenfranchisement of Others" (Thobani 2007, 79, 86).

National Day in each state summons citizens to spectacular displays of tribal loyalty and global citizenship. Bedouin tents line the sides of the roads leading into the capitals, where the media can record their presence, their difference from the *hadar* city slickers, and, above all, their public profession of loyalty to the ruling family.

Both *hadar* and Bedouin tribes claim unadulterated descent from ancient Western Arabia. In societies with little material culture and few, if any, written histories, how can lineage be traced? Some scholars argue that pure tribal lineages have always been a myth because "there has always been interaction among tribes on all levels (including intermarriage) . . . the structural dissolution of the tribes was not consequential to tribal solidarity. Thus, although the economic basis of the social reproduction of tribes had been undermined by change, the sense of tribal identity continued to thrive" (Tibi 1990, 131, 135). This sense of tribal identity is so pervasive that it has survived structural dissolution and socio-economic change in the idea of the tribe.

The idea of the tribe is organic. Over time, tribes and their clans may amalgamate with others to form new tribes or, to the contrary, they may split if they grow too large to administer or if their leaders move, and "a powerful or wealthy man emerges within one of its branches, then imposes his authority over the whole group...It is common for the contemporary name of a clan to be spontaneously linked to prior names" (74). The link to an ancestral name, Bassam Tibi writes, provides the thread of apparent continuity as long as the historicity of the new genealogy is not questioned: "Though chronologically vague, their sense of historical longevity is realistically based on the material evidence of the built environment and local documents...Shaikhs therefore insist that their clans are the 'original, authentic' (*asli*) shaikhly dynasties of their tribes...Partly by their own efforts, therefore, shaikhs and elders embody the permanence as well as the contemporary identities of their tribes" (77). The constructed purity of the rulers' lineage becomes a guarantee for that of their tribe. This is precisely what happened in nineteenth-century Doha.

The story begins in 1847, when Muhammad, son of Thani, one of the leaders in the Al Mu'adid tribe (Al means tribe or family in Arabic, hence Al Mu'adid means the Mu'adid tribe), left Fuwairat for Doha. He and his troops quickly acquired power and prestige on the eastern shore of the Arabian Peninsula. In 1851, the Doha tribe elders appointed Muhammad to mediate a territorial dispute with Bahrain involving the Saudi emir Faisal bin Turki (r. 1843–1865). After successfully negotiating an end to the threat,

Muhammad's new tribal confederation became known as the Al Thani, or the Thani tribe, in honor of Muhammad's father. In 1868, the British recognized Muhammad as the first shaikh of Qatar.

This is not the official version of Al Thani lineage. In his summary of an authorized Qatari account, Edmund O'Sullivan glosses the details in this story, including the change in tribal affiliation. He merely states "the Al Maadhid (or, Mu'adid), a section of the Tameem tribe which originated in Al Washm in the Najd, migrated to the south of the peninsula early in the 18th century, when the region was dominated by the Bani Khalid tribe. In the middle of the century, they moved to Zubara, Ruwais and Fuwairat in the north of the Peninsula. The Al Thani moved from Zubara to Doha in 1847 and made it the capital" (O'Sullivan 2008, 211). In this version of events, Al Mu'adid is a section of Al Tamim (Tameem), considered to be the elite ancestors of all Gulf tribal leaders. Al Mu'adid migrated to the region and then, within a few years and without explanation, the Al Thani emerged as a separate tribal entity that assumed power in nineteenth-century Doha.

The truth is more complicated. The preceding account masks the contingency of tribal affiliations and names. Contingency is erased, and then replaced with kinship and authenticity discourses. The Al Thani are now said to have come from Najd centuries ago. Claiming as their ancestor Qa'qa' ibn 'Amr Al Tamimi, a legendary Arab warrior who helped spread Islam to the Levant, they ignore and gloss over changes in tribal affiliation that complicate the pure blood story.[2] Yet, the traces of other tribal affiliations remain, even if they must be sought in the

Figure 4. 2007 Rulers of the State of Qatar commemorative stamps.

oddest of places. Consider the transition of Muhammad bin Thani of the Al Mu'adid to an Al Thani, as it is celebrated in the 2007 commemoration stamp series entitled "Rulers of Qatar."

Look at these stamps, beginning with the top-right stamp: Shaikh Muhammad bin Thani 1850–1878. To the left we read the name of Shaikh Jasim bin Muhammad Al Thani 1878–1913. Now, in the second row on the right: Shaikh 'Abdallah bin Jasim Al Thani 1913–1949. To the left: Shaikh 'Ali bin 'Abdallah Al Thani 1949–1960. Finally, turn to the third row on the right: Shaikh Ahmad bin 'Ali Al Thani 1960–1972, and to his left: Shaikh Khalifa bin Ahmad Al Thani 1972–1995. The large center image presents the current Emir Shaikh Hamad bin Khalifa Al Thani without name or date. Why does this matter? Let me explain.

The first stamp in the top right-hand corner identifies the first ruler as Shaikh Muhammad bin Thani. There is no tribal affiliation since there is no "Al" (Arabic for tribal family, to be distinguished from al-, indicating the definite article) affixed to his name. He is a tribal leader with the title Shaikh, merely Shaikh Muhammad bin Thani, that is, Muhammad the son of Thani, a common first name for a man, and the tribal Al Mu'adid is omitted. Only two generations are indicated. By the time that his son Jasim takes over in 1878, his father has acquired a new tribal affiliation; his son is now called Shaikh Jasim bin Muhammad *Al* Thani, and the affiliation has stuck.[3]

Some tribes flourish; others may not. In 'Abd al-Rahman Munif's *Cities of Salt*, we read of a tribe invented in a time of plenty but experiencing local powerlessness. After joining the American oil company that has been prospecting in the area previously under his tribe's control, the Bedouin Shaalan feels "compelled in the absence of his father, to establish a new tribe to replace the old one" (Munif 1986, 133). The product of necessity, and with little to offer its new members, this new tribe quickly disappears.

Once a new tribe has been named, the borders around its territory harden and "are portrayed as ancient, immutable, and sacrosanct, especially by politicians, who have a vested interest in the image and reality of permanence and stability ... Keeping borders and security zones in good cognitive repair is therefore comparable to maintaining genealogies in systems where tribes are defined as groups of people descended from a common ancestor" (Weir 2007, 92, 94). Geographic borders equal lineages equal safeguards for a tribe, defining its location, its history, and its blood. The greater the distance from the founding ancestor, the nobler the tribe: "distinctions are drawn according to recent and traceable 'origins' (*asl*)...it is a common put down, for example, to say, 'He can't trace his history'" (56).[4] This could not be said of the restless Al Murrah. Their eponymous ancestor Murrah is said to have married "the progenitress of all his descendants [who] was a *jinnia,* a female spirit" (Cole 1975, 93). This harking back to the source of a tribe in a prehistoric moment is strengthened in its connection to the jinn—supernatural yet human-connected beings—believed by some to be the forebears of desert dwellers.

TRIBAL CLASSES

The incursion of capitalism and globalization in the region has revealed the constructedness of tribes and their lineages. A dramatic, if less visible, change is the transformation of tribal status into social class, splitting the formerly egalitarian tribal society of the desert shaikhdoms into at least five classes.

At the top of the class pyramid is the ruler's family, followed by the tribes that have demonstrated loyalty. Sultan Al-Qassemi writes, "Tribal loyalty continues to be employed even within state borders as a tool of managing populations" (Al-Qassemi 2012). Disloyalty entails loss of status. During the Great Depression and the 1920s' collapse of the date and pearl markets, some tribes fled Qatar for Bahrain, Iran, and Saudi Arabia, where they waited out the crisis in relative comfort. After the discovery of oil and its exploitation in the late 1940s, they returned. During the "years of hunger" between the 1930s and 1950s, a new hierarchy had emerged with the ruling family secure on top (Fromherz 2012, 119). The tribes that stayed are today's elites, and they maintain their status through marriage. The tribes that left during the hard times became second-class citizens, but citizens nonetheless.

Third-class Gulf Arabs are those with Persian connections. They may be either `ajam,[5] Arabs originally from Persia, or *haulas*, Arabs who left the Peninsula, usually to escape tribal feuding, settled in Persia, and then returned to the Arabian shores of the Gulf.[6] One well-placed *haula* told me that his tribe left the central Arabian Peninsula 800 years ago. After living in Emadedeh in Persia for 600 years, his ancestors came to Qatar. Despite two hundred years' residence on the Arabian side of the Gulf, and although neither he nor anyone in his family had ever visited their "home town," he knew that he could not claim to be *asil* because his history contains too much of the Persian.

The `abid, or slaves, constitute the fourth class of native citizens. Africans brought to the region in the past, their class is written on the blackness of their skin. Some of these slaves "became powerful agents of the Sheikh. In fact, slaves were often used as proxy rulers, representatives and informers" (Fromherz 2012, 142). Manumitted in the 1950s, some took their owners' tribal patronymic.[7] They remain racially marked, however, as lower than the other three classes of native citizens.

Below former slaves are the Bedoon. Despite the privilege that birth and blood should bestow, some Gulf Arab tribes are stateless. Their presence has been most evident in Saudi Arabia, the UAE, and in Kuwait, where the Nationality Law of 1959 gave citizenship to sons of Kuwaiti fathers, but it also required that people register to become citizens. At that time, many nomads failed to register because some had not understood "the newly introduced concept of citizenship," and others wanted to hold on "to their traditional pattern of cyclical migration" (Longva 1997, 48, 50). It was only in the 1980s that statelessness became a problem when the oil crisis led governments to restrict citizenship laws and related social goods. States have preferred to ignore the stateless issue.[8] Consequently, until today the Bedoon are claiming the rights that they lost when they did not register as citizens of the new nation-state. In February 2012, Mona Kareem, a female Bedoon blogger, launched the Bedoon Rights website to document a situation in which these stateless people "cannot legally obtain birth, death, marriage or divorce certificates. The same applies to driving licenses, identification cards, and passports. They do not have access to public education, health care, housing or employment. And while they face some of the state's harshest discrimination policies, they have no recourse to the law and its courts. Simply stated, the Bedoon, who are equal to about 10 percent of the Kuwaiti population, do not exist. They have been dehumanized and rendered invisible by government policies coupled with pervasive social stigmatization."[9]

The Kuwaiti Bedoon situation has parallels elsewhere. Citizenship took on significance only when the social and material goods it provided became more evident, but by then it was too late, and tribes' refusal to register ostracized them from the new nation-state. In some cases, the Bedoon may have fewer rights than foreigners. Not surprisingly, the Arab revolutions of 2011 stimulated the Bedoon to mobilize.[10]

CONCLUSION

The spatialization of native citizens distinguishes them from the foreign majority, while also making new tribal class distinctions visible. Living in their own stratified enclaves, citizens settle "according to tribal affiliation... In each tribal village within the city, no matter how small, there is a mosque and a *majlis*... qualified men of the tribe decide on internal matters and the relationship between the tribe and others" (Fromherz 2012, 21, 31).

From tribe to race to class and back to tribe, the idea of the tribe is constantly evolving and self-renewing. In today's Gulf, tribe becomes race for exclusive citizenship; race becomes class for a larger share of the national wealth; wealth subsidizes the production of an essentialized tribal culture, a national culture appropriate for insertion into the twenty-first-century world where these Gulf states wish to play a major role. These transformations of tribe into race and then class—especially the urban, cosmopolitan class—produce the privileged national citizen. This process reveals the interdependence of the tribal and the modern, the building blocks for a new brand that the Arab Gulf states are cultivating in order to broadcast power abroad and retain privilege at home.

CHAPTER FOUR

The Brand

It is necessary to get away from the understanding of tribes as some sort of a medieval form of social organization. Instead, we need to emphasise the process of innovation, inventiveness, vitality and persistence in our analysis of tribal political organization and politicians... Among the wealthy and upper-class milieus of Benghasi, tribal belonging has already changed from denoting a way of life in the past to marking an identity today.

    Huesken 2012

Tribes helped humans survive the last ice age, build farming communities, and, later, cities. Birds flock, fish school, people 'tribe'... The members of your tribe are probably programmed in your cell phone and in your email address book... Tribes are the basic building block of any large human effort... What makes some tribes more effective than others is culture.   Logan, King, and Fisher-Wright 2008

Far from medieval or primitive markers, tribes are modern. Thomas Huesken and Dave Logan alert us to the resilience of tribal structures and affiliations in Libya, and their relevance to leadership in today's multinational corporations. Likewise in the Arab Gulf tribes mark contemporary identities. On the one hand, tribes are passive recipients: globalization has spread and crept into the remotest tribal areas, and opened them up to new media, new ideas, and new people. On the other hand, tribes are hyperactive: oil wealth has fueled ambitions for nationals–tribals to be recognized globally (Comaroff and Comaroff 2009, 122, 123, 182). Each Gulf nation-state has to find ways to distinguish itself from its neighbors while confronting local challenges to newfound wealth and potential power. The mark of distinction, that is also the brand of excellence, is the tribe.

In the early 1980s, the mandate to brand national differences ran up against the need to unite against regional dangers. Of particular concern was Iran, where the Shah had been overthrown in 1979 and replaced with Ayatollah Khomeini's Islamic Republic of Iran. The Shiite message spread throughout the region, a message that resonated well with the restive Shiite populations in the Arab Gulf. Then, in 1980, the Iran-Iraq War broke out, pitting the Cold War superpowers against each other. The tiny, fledgling states had to unite, and in 1981, the Gulf Cooperation Council (GCC) came into being with six member states: Saudi Arabia, Oman, UAE, Qatar, Kuwait, and Bahrain. All were modeled on the European Economic Community. Projecting a collective Gulf identity,[1] the GCC paradoxically provides an umbrella for the consolidation of different local identities that are invariably tribal. Though nation trumps tribe in the quest for international recognition, the idea of the tribe connotes aristocracy, and it remains absolutely salient for symbolic power and wealth distribution at home (Fox, Mourtada-Sabbah, and al-Mutawa 2006, 3, 7).

In June 2012, Shaikh Mohammed bin Rashid Al Maktoum, Vice-President and Prime Minister of the UAE and Ruler of Dubai, invited residents to select a UAE brand logo that would represent "a nation with prestigious political status and an attractive environment, and a unique tourism and culture destination... The UAE is a nation whose citizens enjoy high degrees of national pride, patriotism, unity and a sense of shared belonging and connectedness."[2]

Cultural tourism in the burning barrenness of the Gulf? Nineteenth-century British travelers like Palgrave would not believe their eyes, were they to return to those places they had found so unpalatable. Gone are the hardships (for tourists), and in their place are previously undreamt-of luxuries. And, of course, the sun in winter. The importance of tourism in the regional economies has grown with the awareness that oil income must be supplemented and ultimately replaced. "Governments use tourism as a major anchor for economic diversification" writes the editor of *Khaleej Times* on May 6, 2013, "tourism in the Emirates is growing significantly faster than the world GDP growth average, contributing an impressive 14 percent to the UAE economy in 2012—compared to the global trend of 9 percent—and expected to rise by 3.2 percent in 2013... Qatar is also moving ahead with its $65 billion investment plan that focuses on the state's hosting of the 2022 FIFA World Cup."

Tourism matters also in cultures that are looking for hypermodern ways to shape new national identities and to spectacularize themselves to the world. "I see the tourist as providing an ethnography of modernity" writes Mike Robinson. "As a dominant force of contemporary global mobility tourism provides us with a useful framework to understand the changing forms and formats of heritage...Tourism as a phenomenon of modernity (merging into 'hypermodernity')³ provides insights into the wider condition of culture and society" (Robinson 2011, 216). In the Gulf Arab states, cultural tourism projects target foreigners and locals alike, the former for pleasure and the latter for pride, patriotism, unity, and a sense of shared belonging and connectedness.

What is this shared sense of belonging and connectedness that Shaikh Mohammed bin Rashid Al Maktoum touted in his call for a new national brand? Is it not a thinly veiled appeal to a timeless tribal identity, the glue that sustains citizen identity, loyalty, and success? Yes. Each Gulf state is striving to create a unique tourism destination for outsiders while strengthening a sense of shared belonging for its native citizens. Their preferred brand might be: "Tribal modern—Yes, we can!"

Increasingly visible, the tribal modern brand markets cutting edge projects, even though the word "tribal" may not be used explicitly. The theme of the 2011 Sharjah Islamic Arts Festival was "Tradition and Modernity." In July 2012, the UAE Post issued special stamps featuring the annual Liwa Date Festival, a "distinguished heritage event and tourist attraction...The date is a classic symbol of Arabian *heritage* and it is important to highlight its role and benefits to the *modern* generation," said Ibrahim Bin Karam of Emirates Post Group (my emphasis).⁴ How does this UAE tribal modern brand differ from that found in other Gulf countries with identical cultures and histories?

AUTHENTICITY

Gulf Arabs are pursuing what historians Eric Hobsbawm and Terence Ranger call "invented traditions." Like other new nations, Gulf countries invent traditions "not because old ways are no longer available or viable, but because they are deliberately not used or adapted" (Hobsbawm and Ranger 1983, 8). A tabula rasa has to be created on which invented traditions will: a) establish or symbolize social cohesion or the membership of groups; b) establish or legitimize institutions, status or relations of authority; and c) allow for "the inculcation of beliefs, value systems and conventions of behaviour" (9). Most importantly, invented traditions create a historical narrative that fosters "the corporate sense of *superiority* of elites ... nationalism [becomes] a substitute for social cohesion through ... collective group representations" (10, 13, 303). In the Gulf, invented traditions provide regimes with symbolic capital that undergirds elite privilege within new national borders; they help to convert oil wealth into nationally legible cultural capital, and they project socio-national cohesion with an emphasis on tribal purity.

Invented traditions mitigate the newness of these new nations by claiming to be "rooted in the remotest antiquity ... human communities so 'natural' as to require no definition other than self-assertion" (14). National Day celebrations carefully segregate national citizens from migrant workers. The Bedouin don distinctive tribal dress and perform spectacles of loyalty to royal families said to trace their lineage back to the Prophet Muhammad's tribe in Western Arabia. Islamic authenticity is one of the layers of the palimpsest of invented traditions that create cultural patrimony and, above all, authenticity, the word constantly invoked to refer to tribal lineage and status.

The obsession with authenticity recalls the battle cry of Arab anticolonial movements from the 1930s to the 1960s, but with a difference. For the resisting Mediterranean Arabs, authenticity meant a return to status quo ante, a moment before the arrival of the Europeans in the late eighteenth century. The hope invested in authenticity was recuperative: decades, and in some cases centuries, of outside intervention could be shaken off, and native subjects could regain a primordial identity that had lain dormant throughout foreign intervention. But the project failed, and failure produced disappointment, anger, and alienation. The Algerians who had believed that expelling the French would spirit away their language, culture, and political influence soon realized the futility of such hopes. Algerian, French, Berber, Arab, and Muslim cultural and linguistic identities jostled for a place in the authenticity hierarchy. Sixty years later, the existential crisis persists and continues to fuel socio-political crises.

If authenticity was militantly utopian in the Mediterranean anticolonial struggles; in the Arab Gulf it has been culturally aggressive. Not only was the British colonial presence less intrusive, but Britain is also credited with bringing Pax Britannica to a region embroiled in piracy and internecine warfare. Part of the difference derives from the style of colonial rule. While Mediterranean Arabs were chafing under the yoke of imperial rule, Gulf shaikhs retained a significant degree of autonomy from the British. As already noted, the British had little interest in these inhospitable lands beyond assuring the safety of their people and the security of goods traveling between the British Isles

and the British Raj. There is also a difference in resource potential. Unlike Mediterranean Arab countries that fell into political and socio-economic disarray after independence, Arab Gulf
states discovered incalculable natural resources that eased the
daunting transition to national self-rule and rendered shaikhly
authority less precarious because all native citizens—in varying degrees—shared in the wealth. Whatever expertise they
lacked—whether due to poor educational facilities or lack of
experts for the work required—they imported.[5] Far from suffering the labor and brain drain besetting other Arab countries,
native citizens stayed put and imported droves of foreigners who
transformed their deserts into cosmopolitan capitals. Although
many summer in London, few live there. Elites comfortably
straddle the tribal authentic and the hypermodern. In this space
the modern, the tribal, and the national meet. Out of this space
of multiple borders emerges the brand.

THINKING THROUGH THE INTERSTICES: THE *BARZAKH*

Borders separate foreigner from native, men from women, east
from west, tribal from modern. But they also connect one to
the other. How can we think this separating/connecting line
as another kind of space, a space where seeming opposites are
simultaneously and reciprocally constituted?

A different way of knowing is required. Some call it border
thinking. The South American subaltern scholar Walter Mignolo
theorizes border thinking as an explicit challenge to dichoto-
mized ways of knowing. Emphasizing the multiplicity of knowl-

edge systems produced around the edges of colonial power, Mignolo demonstrates how border thinking challenges colonial epistemology and intersects with different knowledge systems. Those marginalized by and struggling with the colonial-modern engage in a border thinking that recognizes, defines, and accents the line separating indigenous cultures and knowledge systems from the colonial-modern (Mignolo 2000). It is there, in the space of intersection among multiple knowledge systems, that we can locate the tribal and the colonial-modern. To understand how such a space functions in the mutual constitution of the tribal and the modern, it needs to be broadened so that the various entities in this equation converge, even while remaining distinct. It is only their seemingly contradictory yet totally undiluted convergence that releases the potential for their dynamic interaction.

I call this liminal space the *barzakh*, a Qur'anic term that variously designates the metaphysical space between life and the hereafter and also the physical space between sweet and salt waters.[6] A spatial, temporal, and figurative term, the *barzakh* is mentioned in the Qur'an three times. In Q 23:100, the dead find themselves in "a *barzakh* until the day they are raised." In Q 25:53, Allah "mixed the two seas, the one potable and sweet, the other salty and bitter; and between them He placed a *barzakh*." A later verse repeats the mixing of the two seas, but adds that their meeting is also their separation, for "between them a *barzakh* they cannot overpass. Which then of your Lord's favors can you deny? Out of these two seas come forth pearls and coral" (Q 55:19–22). These sea verses describe either a miracle or an apparent impossibility. How can two great bodies of water meet without commingling and thus diluting into bland sameness? What is the nature of this liquid barrier that it produces something new and extraordinary?

The waters referred to in these two verses probably describe the sweet and the salt waters around the island of Bahrain—Bahrain in Arabic means "two seas." Even today, salt water incongruously overlays the sweet. It results from the flowing of prehistoric streams of fresh water through fossil aquifers from the underground of the Arabian Peninsula into the seabed around Bahrain. That sweet water has continued until today to retain its separateness from the salt water.[7]

It is a puzzle and a process that has fascinated writers, artists, and mystics. In Abdulaziz Al Mahmoud's *The Corsair* we read about this *barzakh* that has perennially kept the salt and sweet waters of Bahrain separate. A British captain is negotiating with Shaikh Salman Al Khalifa, the ruler of Bahrain in the early nineteenth century, when he is given sweet water to drink. Delighted at the taste of sweet rather than brackish water generally available in the Gulf towns, he asks for more. Shaikh Salman orders one of his men to oblige the guest and, to the amazement of the British captain and his crew, a man "strips off his clothes, dives smoothly into the sea and returns, a few minutes later, with the bottle full of [fresh] water" (Al Mahmoud 2012, 72).

Why do these two seas not overpass? Because in the very instant that they connect they disconnect; they are fully mixed and present in that space but also absent. The *barzakh* holds these and also other opposing elements in constant equilibrium, adjusting with their alterations so that one will never overwhelm the other (see Belghazi 2001).

Egyptian artist Ahmed Mustafa has created this calligraphic rendition of the *barzakh* by bringing together mirror images of

Figure 5. Barzakh painting by Ahmed Mustafa (courtesy of Ahmed Fenoon).

Qur'anic verses 55:19–20. The verse and its reflection are split and brought together by the alif and lam, the "la," which is the Arabic word for no or not. The two lams, doubled in the reflection, establish the edges of the *barzakh*, the space intervening between the mirrored verses, while the two alifs provide the lines that reach across it.

According to the thirteenth-century mystic and philosopher Ibn ʿArabi, the Arabian Gulf and in it, Bahrain, is the quintessential *barzakh*. In the rare commingling of these two waters, he writes, unique pearls are created: "the jewel in the mother of pearl is formed of the sweet and the salt waters."[8] Records found in ancient graves in Bahrain attest to the fact that for seven thousand years, the bed of the Gulf has produced the world's most precious pearls.[9] Moreover, unlike other pearls formed either in sweet water or in salt water, Gulf pearls—mentioned in the Qur'anic passage cited above—are produced through the seemingly miraculous coming together of these two elements, unmixed but always mixing. The perfect pearl is the product, and also the icon, of the Gulf *barzakh*.

This mixing and separation happens not only in the Gulf, but also in other bodies of differently constituted water where such barriers prevent dilution. Recent oceanographic researchers have examined what happens in the *barzakh* space where the warmer, more saline, and less dense Mediterranean waters meet the Atlantic Ocean.[10]

The epistemological *barzakh* in which the tribal and the modern meet and separate has inspired Bahraini writer Farid Ramadan. In 2000, he published a novel about a man's suspension between life and death that he entitled *Al-barzakh. Najma fi safar* (The Barzakh: A Star on the Journey; see Ramsay 2005, 140–45). The hero of Dubai's Ibrahim Mubarak's "Grief of the Night Bird" describes the coexistence of the tribal and the modern in his life, equally at ease with desert falcons and the "city and its hubbub and its new ways. Thus in the winter he roamed the deserts to hunt game animals, while in the summer he was a frequenter of cafes and nightclubs, and saw nothing wrong with that" (Johnson-Davies 2009, 54).

Only in the *barzakh* can the dynamic of cultural continuity and change be discerned. In the Gulf, tribal societies long on the edge of world history have recently commanded attention to their role in the world. The tribal and the modern in today's Gulf states cannot be disentangled. In the fifty-year *barzakh* linking and separating the pre-oil shaikhdoms and today's nation-states, each is shaping the other in a dynamic, cultural-political field in which apparently contradictory states remain in balance, the tribal does not compromise with the modern, nor does the modern erase the tribal. Is this possible? By Aristotelian logic, no; by *barzakh* logic, yes.

Shaikhdoms with their millennial tribal structure, stratifications, and indigenous cosmologies are fully engaged in the hypermodern world hubs of travel, commerce, and politics, using "indigenous cosmology to incorporate new technologies into a coherent idea system to enact a viable social fabric…both globalism and tribalism arise to 'organize coherence' at different nested levels within larger crisscrossing networks" (Fox, Mourtada-Sabbah, and al-Mutawa 2006, 9, 26). The dynamic of globalism and tribalism narrates tribal history otherwise and provides another way to think about the incursion of the new into the flow of desert time. Less teleological and cataclysmic, modernity becomes just another encounter, another moment that dots the stream of time.

Viewing history through a *barzakh* lens reveals the ways in which encounters survive in the indelible effects that they have produced, even if these effects are buried under the crushing weight of history tomes. World historian Marshall Hodgson blames "the dead hand of tradition" (Hodgson 1993, 86) for obscuring the dynamic of cultural encounters and the traces they leave behind. Encounters are not about who wins and who loses and disappears, according to Hodgson, but about how the coming together of differences reveals "the great commitments and loyalties that human beings have borne" (76). It is in the meetings of these diverse and competing commitments and loyalties that new opportunities are created, new realities born. Convergences between different societies shaped by their heritage and their commitments survive in some form in the palimpsest of history, however faint the traces and however determined the winner to eliminate them.

CONCLUSION

Barzakh logic is not unique to the Arab Gulf. Between different and competing elements, there will always be a *barzakh*. Without it, differences would overwrite one another or else dilute into bland sameness. It is the civilizational *barzakh* of the tribal modern that divides and defines differences in mutually constitutive and newly productive ways. While the generative space of the *barzakh* is at once physical and metaphysical, cultural and civilizational, it is also, critically, epistemological. *Barzakh* thinking lingers in all liminal states of separation, connection, and transformation. It is crucial to the Arab Gulf brand. Thinking the imbrication of the tribal with the modern through a cultural *barzakh* explains the creation of multiple Arab Gulf brands. The next three chapters discuss how individual states are elaborating and marketing the brand.

CHAPTER FIVE

Building the Brand

A nation without a past is a nation without a present
or a future. Thanks to God, our nation has a flourishing civilization, deep-rooted in this land for many
centuries. These roots will always flourish and bloom
in the glorious present of our nation and in its
anticipated future.

> Shaikh Zayed Bin Sultan Al Nahyan, the UAE's
> founding father[1]

I am driving through downtown Dubai in 2008 with a sinking
feeling. There is something disappointing about the glass and
steel skyline, the traffic jams, and the theme parking of the Orient.
This is and is not the Empty Quarter with its fearsome desert
stretching days across waterless wastes. The orientalist's idyll
has vanished behind rows of flashy hotels and multinational corporations. The flourishing civilization that Abu Dhabi's Shaikh
Zayed Bin Sultan Al Nahyan claimed was deep-rooted in the
land for many centuries hides its traces behind "a strange medley
of Wall Street and Disneyland, of American and Arabian symbolism. Dubai represents itself as the ambassador of the future

Arab *umma*" (Abifares 2005). Ambassador and foremost icon of the region and the future Arab *umma*, this is how Dubai markets itself to the world.

But there is more to this city and others in the Arab Gulf than simple pastiche of Arab and Western fragments forecasting the future of the Arab *umma*, or Arab nation writ large. Behind the hype and the closed doors of Gulf Arabs' homes tribal values and norms shape the ways in which modernity is lived.

During the past twenty years, Arab Gulf countries have competed to produce the most dramatic skylines and cutting-edge designs.[2] Dubai's 828-meter space-age Burj Khalifa dwarfs New York's Empire State Building. Qatar's Museum of Islamic Art is a stunning hybrid of cubism and Islamic motifs that the Chinese-American architect I. M. Pei derived from iconic buildings in North Africa and Islamic Spain. To showcase his architectural jewel, he planted his vision on a man-made island just off the Corniche. Many such instant islands, including Dubai's Jumeirah Palm, Kuwait's Green Island, Qatar's Pearl, and Bahrain's Bay Development, are popping up out of the shallow waters of the Gulf. They feature importantly in urban planning.

Reclaimed land increases national territory, creates luxury waterfront properties, and provides a stage for spectacular experiments in international living. On Dubai's Jumeirah Palm, for example, "investors can choose from a range of stylistic options: Arabic, Mediterranean, European, Contemporary, Caribbean, Floridian, Ranch, New Mexican, Bali, Spanish, Italian, and the oddly titled 'One Style'... 'modern' interior and an 'Arabic' exterior characterized by either domes and arches or decorative wind towers" (Mitchell 2007, 131, 133). These building projects offer what architect Kevin Mitchell calls "a themed experience that...

freely interprets and invents traditions [with] little beyond the façade treatment" (135). Authentic and inauthentic elements are pastiched together in such a way that the "architects' fantasy turns out to be a fiction marketed as a fact" (136). Invented traditions? The words trip lightly off the tongues of PR agents. While most architects are satisfied with their lucrative fantasies, some are searching in the local culture for the elements that will create a modern urban landscape true to its desert context. Tradition is the desert, and the emblem of the desert is the tribe.

In this chapter, I examine two contrasting examples of tribal modern architecture in Qatar. The first by a French starchitect features a fantastic braiding of the tribal modern brand in the future national museum. The second by a local architect combines design elements from around the Gulf region to build a credible traditional-tribal market for hypermodern consumption.

NATIONAL MUSEUMS

National museums publicize country brands. Whereas European museums devote much wall and floor space to the art and material culture that have distinguished their nations, post-independence states in Africa and Asia use their national museums to project a new, "authentic" (namely, free of European influence) image. A relatively recent phenomenon, Asian, African, and Latin American national museums since the nineteenth century were often tied to colonial projects. The greater the national history, the worthier the nation of European "patronage." Patronage entailed "help" in organizing those elements that made the country unique (at the cost of precious items shipped back to the British Museum or the Louvre or the Prado). Exhibits featured archaeological, ethnographic, and traditional artifacts that highlighted the country's distinctiveness and qualification to be placed on the world map.

Each Arabian Peninsula country has a national museum. Whereas Saudi Arabia's museum in Riyadh highlights the nation's role in the history and spread of Islam,[3] the Gulf states have used their national museums to broadcast their histories, their similar histories. In 1973, for example, Qatar's Shaikh Khalifa commissioned a British archaeological study for a national museum to be housed in the Fariq Al Salatah Palace. After the first phase, the government appointed a committee of local and international researchers to establish the ruling family's links to the various periods represented in the museum. But the collection of artifacts and oral narratives confronted what one researcher described as "deeply conflicting local myths of the state. It is hard to reconcile a monarchist ideology (for the ruler) with a capitalist ideology (for the merchants) with a social entitlement ideology (for the population). The tensions inherent in this project have not been resolved. They manifest themselves in a deep distrust of research, a tendency to take refuge in the more distant past and in *turath*, or cultural heritage" (Crystal 1990, 163–64).

Although Jill Crystal was writing over twenty years ago, the distrust of national research persists, as does the issue of what constitutes appropriate content for a national museum. A way to deal with this problem is to minimize the importance of the contents, which are, after all, hard to come by, since objects, particularly art objects, in the pre-oil days, were simple and few. Consequently, the new national museum in Qatar, like its equivalent in Abu Dhabi, will be all about the buildings, and in the process the passive spectacular will replace the active intellectual focus.[4]

The architectural elements of the UAE and Qatar national museums will narrate the history of the country from prehistoric times. The museumological historiography will conclude with the transformation of shaikhdom into nation-state. Foreigners were commissioned to design both hypermodern buildings that will deliver individual, nationally distinguishable narratives to promote each nation's tribal modern brand.[5] British Norman Foster's design of Abu Dhabi's Zayed National Museum highlights the Emirati obsession with falcons, while a desert rose and caravanserai inspired French Jean Nouvel's design for Qatar's National Museum. Both museums will be built on the shore of the Gulf, and their nestled waterfront location will bring together desert tribal symbols with the sea that provided pre-oil *hadari* Arabs with their meager sustenance.

"To look far forward, you have to look far back," Norman Foster once said, echoing Sheikh Zayed Bin Sultan Al Nahyan's slogan. His design for the future Abu Dhabi national museum will feature five high-tech soaring pavilions, representing the feathers of a falcon's wing.[6] Respect for the past, he explained, reveals national uniqueness. In the Gulf, Foster found an "architecture without architects [that transformed] a hostile, barren desert into wonderful spaces" with lovely wind towers that were cutting-edge technology and not merely decoration. Inspired by anonymous predecessors, Foster worked with nature to come up with a design that "celebrates the culture and traditions of the country" through flight and falcons.[7]

Jean Nouvel[8] followed a similar trajectory. His design will reflect "the vanishing bedouin cultures of Qatar in an effort to embrace the realities of a rapidly urbanizing society, and maintain a connection to this fading world in which the country sprang. The starting points of the design began with the desert rose, which are tiny formations which crystallize below the desert's surface. Made primarily from steel and concrete which will be locally sourced/fabricated, the new building will be constructed from dozens of interlocking disk-like forms varying in curvature and diameter, suggestive of the blade-like petals of the desert rose ... a manifestation of the Qatari identity, through a building appearing as if it is growing out of the ground [...] The museum will be surrounded by a 1.2 million square foot landscaped park, which interprets the Qatari desert landscape."[9] And in this park he will place the museum, which in form and tone recalls not so much roses as spacecraft.

A postindustrial gesture to intergalactic exploration and travel that is also a nostalgic evocation of Bedouin culture, Nouvel's museum etches a cluster of desert roses growing out of the desert landscape. What could articulate the *barzakh* brand more eloquently than this simultaneous linking of Qataris to a lunar future and to their desert roots? The museum will elaborate a distinctive identity permeated with the *barzakh* motif: it is neither Gulf nor Western, tribal nor modern, and yet both and, above all, something else. Since Qatari culture, with its impoverished pearling and nomadic history, has few material objects of great interest, the museum interior will focus on the intangible. Oral histories will be relayed on digital screens lining the walls.[10]

Nouvel articulates his vision explicitly in terms that can only be described as tribal modern: "a nomadic people builds its capital city and talks about it through this emblematic monument built with the most contemporary construction tools (steel, glass, and fire concrete), and will communicate through high-definition cinema, incorporating visitors' movements into its museogra-

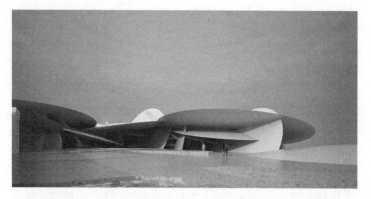

Figure 6. Qatar National Museum north view up close: one of the spaceship/desert roses (credit granted by Ateliers Jean Nouvel and Artefactory).

phy: this museum is a modern-day caravanserai. From there you leave the desert and you return from it bringing back treasured images that remain forever engraved on your memory. This is more than just a metaphor. The national museum of Qatar will become Qatar's voice of culture, delivering a message about the metamorphosis of modernity and the beauty that happens when the desert meets the sea."[11] A modern caravanserai that morphs modernity at the intersection of desert and sea, the National Museum will create the desert affect on the shores of the Gulf. Visitors will wander around in the *barzakh* that separates yet connects three distinct elements: the desert, the sea, and the new shining city across the Bay. In the form of a desert-rose spaceship it will interweave the tribal and the modern.

Even if Nouvel's statement may not ultimately be legible in the material form he designs and others construct, it is clear that he wants—or, has been asked—to build the tribal modern brand. In its advertisement of the museum, the Qatar Museums Authority alludes to space, speed, and futurity when it promises future international museum visitors "a dialogue about rapid change and modernization. [The building] gives concrete expression to the identity of a nation in movement."[12]

The two Arab Gulf museums of Abu Dhabi and Qatar brand and promote national distinctiveness. They construct a vision of the nation that citizens, foreign residents, and visitors can consume. But they are not the only museums to do so. The Museum of Islamic Art also serves a national *qua* religious function. It elaborates Qatar's "status as a leading member of the Muslim community of states, reminding us of its Wahhabi heritage, its close ties to Saudi Arabia and the holy centers of the Muslim faith, and its deep roots in the cultural traditions of the whole Middle East."[13] Although the Museum of Islamic Art does not display a single object made in Qatar, its location and its priceless collection make an Islamic statement about Qatar's leadership within the contemporary Muslim *umma*.

These museums spectacularize progress, conjoining the global modern with local, tribal culture. Affective vehicles for refiguring and shaping new national identities, they fix what had been fluid and uncertain. Designed and built by foreign labor, they instill pride and instruct tribal citizens how to live "in a global society ... to tell a new story, one that breaks with a long history of regional decline" (Ouroussoff 2010).

VERNACULAR ARCHITECTURE

Another way to instill pride in the nation and to tell a new story is to challenge the accepted notion that the region lacks its own art and architecture. This is what Qatari artist-engineer Muhammad ʿAli ʿAbdullah has done in Suq Waqif, where he wove together *hadar* and Bedouin cultures in a new neighborhood in the heart of Doha.[14]

Unlike the museums' high-profile architects, Muhammad ʿAli is not internationally known. He told me his intriguing story over several months. After his return from America in 1985, with a BFA from the University of Toledo, the government gave him a house.[15] It was the kind of house introduced into the region during the 1960s and 1970s that was part of the "early modernization efforts that didn't take local needs and traditions into account."[16] Muhammad ʿAli complained that this "villa" with its eight balconies and large windows allowed the world to look in on his privacy and invited the heat of the blazing sun into the cool interior. Instead of putting up with the inconvenience, he decided to build a traditional house. Not quite sure what that might be, he threw himself into researching local building designs.

"Gulf architecture," he told me when we first met, "is everywhere so similar you'd think it's one person who designed buildings on both shores of the Gulf Pond."

He insisted on the word "Pond" to make his point that ideas are easily exchanged in such a small, contained region.

"From the earliest times," he explained, "people crossed from one side to the other to escape wars and natural disasters. They did not seek refuge by land since both coasts are cut off from their hinterland by natural barriers: mountains on the Iranian side and the forbidding desert on the Arabian side. Sea travel was considered safer than land. The travelers leaving for Mecca and the Hajj across the Empty Quarter bade their loved ones farewell with little confidence that they would return; those setting sail for Zanzibar were less fearful. While the journey to the African island was 2,000 kilometers, the Hajj route was only 1,000 kilometers, but it was fraught with perils."

Muhammad 'Ali is *'ajami*. Of Persian ancestry, he was more familiar than most Qataris with the Iranian shore of the Gulf Pond. "Construction materials around the Pond are the same. In the north, they are of mud because places like Kuwait are located on the silt plains of the Euphrates estuary. In the south, houses are built of stone, *fesht* (bedrock stone found under coral reefs on which fish and shellfish feed) or *farush* (coral stone) or *salafa* (calcareous sedimentary rock). The ceilings are generally made of *mangrur* (a net composed of strips of painted bamboo) held in place by *chandal* (rope-bound mangrove poles imported from Zanzibar)."[17]

Traveling throughout the region, Muhammad 'Ali pieced together the elements of a traditional house. It was his answer to the derogatory assumption that the Gulf does not have a distinctive architectural style. The uniformity of Gulf architecture inspired the design for his own home: carved wooden doors; rooms around a *haush* or central courtyard; no outside windows; whitewashed walls to deflect the heat of the sun. He included a *majlis*, or men's meeting room, open to the street so that passersby can see if he is receiving and they may enter without knocking. Decorations seamlessly synthesize the ubiquitous geometric patterns particular to the ancient Arabian aesthetic with Persian floral motifs ('Abdullah 2010).

"Gulf architecture," he continued, "emerged out of ancient trading networks that connected people, gave them new ideas and taught them techniques they assimilated and appropriated. Gulf shipbuilders had for centuries ordered teak from the jun-

Figure 7. Interior of Muhammad ʿAli's house decorated for his daughter's wedding.

gles of Calicut that they brought back to the Gulf to be built into dhows. At a certain point in this relationship, the people of Calicut took over the process and built ships according to Gulf specifications. With time these ships were said to be Calicut originals that had influenced Gulf dhows. The Gulf originals disappeared, taking with them their networked, multicultural past."

This is how a *discourse* hegemonic functions: The history of borrowings, appropriations, and contestations disappears. This process has recurred throughout Islamic history: "We think of Bedouin notions as 'surviving' while Iranian ones 'influence' that later culture from outside," writes historian Marshall Hodgson, "The Arabic culture of the High Caliphate then takes on two traits: a) suddenness; b) a derivative character, as largely 'borrowed.' What a difference in tone, if rather we should look at the problems posed by an overlay of Arabic 'borrowing' upon Iranian and Syriac 'survivals'... a culture appears as a pattern of life-ways received among mutually recognized family groups... Historical change is continuous and all traditions are open and in motion, by the very necessity of the fact that they are always in internal imbalance" (Hodgson 1993, 83, 89). Internal imbalance rather than external hierarchy is Hodgson's paradigm for re-thinking cultures in terms of flows and patterns of lifeways. Borrowings and survivals find acknowledgment because all forms exist in a state of internal imbalance. Instead of hegemonic erasure and subaltern protest, a dynamic process is produced. This dynamic process distinguishes the *bar-zakh* of tribal modern civilizational encounters. It reveals the traces that inform Gulf architecture, this architecture without architects.

NATIONALIZING VERNACULAR ARCHITECTURE

Muhammad 'Ali's house attracted the attention of state urban planners on the lookout for examples of vernacular architecture to renew parts of downtown Doha. Muhammad 'Ali was commissioned to design the national mosque and to restore fortress palaces (more like large mud houses than palaces), including the 1860s palace of Qatar's founder Shaikh Jasim bin Muhammad Al Thani, the 1906 palace of Shaikh Jasim's son Abdallah, and the 1917 palace of Shaikh Jasim's grandson Hamad. Shaikh Jasim's palace is the product of Muhammad 'Ali's research and imagination, because the original structure was razed to the ground in the 1960s.

Figure 8. Muhammad ʻAli under one of the Shaikh Jasim Palace mosque domes.

He was instructed to use original building materials so that no future visitors examining the site could say that this was not Shaikh Jasim's palace. He was, however, compelled to use concrete to carry the weight of the forty-four domes, and he was given permission to air-condition the complex.

Dwarfing all these projects was his most important commission to design a concept for a traditional market to be located on the site of an earlier market in the 164,000-square-meter area that used to hold old Doha. Armed with British World War II aerial photographs of the area and four of his own acrylic paintings depicting his childhood memories of Doha, he met with officials from the Emiri Diwan. They were impressed.

Figure 9. Construction of Shaikh Jasim's palace as viewed from author's apartment.

"Start tomorrow!"

And he did.

But where exactly had the old market been? He knew the general area, but he wanted to confirm the precise perimeter of pre-oil Doha. Above all, he needed to know where the buying and selling had taken place. He concentrated on a neighborhood filled with ramshackle shops run by South and Southeast Asians. During the 1970s and 1980s, some poor Qatari shopkeepers had also worked there. Mr. Al Emadi, the CEO of Siddiqi International Group, told me that in 1983 he had taken over his father's 3.5-square-meter `abaya* shop in that neighborhood. It was from this tiny place in the old market that he had launched his multimillion-dollar `abaya* franchise.[18]

Figure 10. Suq Waqif in 1955 and 1960.

These 1955 and 1960 images of the predecessors to Suq Waqif show rows of shops with awnings lining the street. Far from a traditional, pedestrian, covered market, Suq Waqif was an urban commercial district; it even had car access. There was little here to inspire the building of a traditional market that could become a source of national pride.

Because at first he could find little reliable historical documentation, Muhammad 'Ali interviewed old shopkeepers for memory fragments. During his wanderings from store to store, he kept looking for scraps of information that might help him start. One day, he came across a sack filled with documents of sale and loan, as well as letters dating back to the nineteenth century. The shopkeeper let him take the sack, not understanding why these dusty, crumbling papers might be of any value. Muhammad 'Ali had found a treasure.[19]

Sifting through the piles of paper and filing them into archival folders to return to the owner, he lit upon the clue. A letter dated some day in 1888 referred to the wall of Doha. This was the first he had heard of such a wall. Research revealed that in 1888 Shaikh Zayed bin Khalifa of Abu Dhabi had killed the son of Qatar's Shaikh Jasim bin Muhammad Al Thani (r. 1878–1913) during a struggle between the two shaikhs for control of the lucrative pearl market (O'Sullivan 2008, 271; Lorimer 1984, 821). Shaikh Jasim mobilized his militia to retaliate. Knowing that when he and his men left Doha the city would be left unprotected, Shaikh Jasim built a wall. He won the battle and no longer needed the wall. It fell into disrepair because the stones and loose sand mortar used for construction in the region require constant, annual upkeep. They were not kept up. A century later, all trace of the wall had disappeared. Armed with the shopkeeper's letter, Muhammad 'Ali dug around the area where the wall might have been. Buried beneath a century of sand, he stumbled upon the foundations of the wall.

The next step in this archaeological-architectural project was to locate the exact area where a market might have been. He assumed that it would have been along the *kharis*, or flashflood drainage channel, that used to mark the center of most habitations in the Arabian Peninsula. The *kharis* ran through the middle of town because flash floods had to be quickly funneled into a single channel and disposed of lest they submerge the dwellings. The *kharis* was less erased than the ramparts had been, so Muhammad 'Ali could easily trace its course. He situated the market within the perimeter of the old city walls and along the axis of the *kharis*. Having located the center of the settlement, he had made visible the *hadari* half of the culture underlying the creation of Suq Waqif.

Next, he wanted to know how the Bedouin had interacted with the *hadar* townsfolk. In nineteenth-century Doha, houses were built at a slight distance from the *kharis*, on a rise above the dangerous floodwaters. In the space between the houses and the channel, the desert Bedouin daily set up their wares. They stood on the banks of the *kharis* during the day, and then at night they packed up and returned home to the desert surrounding the town. These temporary stands (*waqafa* in Arabic means to stand) gave the market its name, Suq Waqif, or Standing Market, that is, the market where Bedouin vendors stood during the day.

We have a vivid image of the original market from a visitor's report. In his 1865 *Narrative of a Year's Journey through Central and Eastern Arabia*, William Palgrave described the market in Bedaa' (now, Bid'a is a neighborhood in Doha) in colorful terms: "a long narrow and dirty market place; some Bahreyn shopkeepers and artisans ply their business on a small scale; for the rest, Bedaa' consists of a mass of little narrow dingy houses, separated by irregular lanes. The total amount of its inhabitants when on land, which is not often the case, reaches about six thousand." Neighboring Doha at that time was about half the size of Bedaa', and its houses "are even lower or meaner than at Bedaa', and the market place is narrower and dirtier" (cited in Crystal 1990, 28).

Palgrave's description of Suq Waqif in the early 1860s could not be more graphic or dismissive: a tiny, dirty market serving a total population of about three thousand. Nor had it changed much by 1940 when the British Political Resident wrote that the "*suq* consisted of mean fly-infested hovels, the roads were dusty tracks, there was no electricity, and the people had to fetch their water in skins and cans from wells two or three miles outside the town" (Fromherz 2012, 1). What a striking difference between that market and the current Suq Waqif that instead recalls boutique versions of Cairo's Khan al-Khalili, the Ahmadiya Suq in Damascus, or the Marrakesh Medina.

Muhammad 'Ali knew this history, but he also knew how the market had functioned. Placing the new shops along the *kharis*, he included this Bedouin element in his design in order to accommodate both parts of Qatar's cultural-tribal past. *Hadar* and Bedouin tribal accents commingled and conjoined but did not erase each other. *Barzakh* logic prevailed. Further, the market, like Shaikh Jasim's palace, was to be built with local materials brought in from skyscraper construction sites.

Although Muhammad 'Ali does not claim to have renovated something material that had been there before, that is how many others see it. Opened in 2006, two years before the instant island of the Pearl and the Museum of Islamic Art, Suq Waqif is marketed in tourist and promotional websites as "one of the most traditional souqs of the region that dates back to ancient times."[20] While some gush about the "restoration," others are contemptuous. In his article about SUCQ, a Doha-based

Figure 11. Suq Waqif 2010 (photo by Jonathan Cross).

comedian troupe, Peter Savodnik dismisses Suq Waqif with his casual "fake-old-looking."[21]

Suq Waqif, however, is more complicated than this authentic–inauthentic binary. Situated in the affect *barzakh*, this simulacrum is both and neither. Unlike the alienating repro-cultures in developing countries produced for tourist consumption,[22] Suq Waqif has a critical local role to play beyond capital accumulation. In this city of salt that knows little of its past, there are no special pockets of authentic local culture that the curious can discover and to which the locals can retreat. However, even if both *hadar* and Bedouin material cultures have all but disappeared, the feeling of something lost has not. It is this feeling that the market has restored not only for tourists but also for native citizens. It is remarkable how thoroughly this simulacrum—this copy without an original—has displaced its own recent past.

Few wonder where the old men, now comfortably ensconced on high benches, used to smoke their narguilehs before builders squeezed the long, narrow smoking room with its colorful carpets into a side alley.

Muhammad 'Ali is delighted that his creation has been received as a restoration. Suq Waqif, he hoped, would provide a new home for the local population. For the old poet who comes every Thursday, the market alleviates the pain of loss and nostalgia for a bygone time. It does not matter that Suq Waqif is new; what matters is the affect of authenticity it produces.[23]

So successful was Suq Waqif that in 2010 it was short-listed for the prestigious Aga Khan Award for Architecture. The award, launched in 1977 to counter the westernization of architecture in Muslim countries and to infuse buildings with indigenous, often Islamic content, "recognizes examples of architectural excellence that encompass contemporary design, social housing, community improvement and development, restoration, re-use, and area conservation [...] Particular attention is given to building schemes that use local resources and appropriate technology in an innovative way, and to projects likely to inspire similar efforts elsewhere."[24] The key ingredients are area conservation, local resources, and appropriate technology. With its welcoming narguileh cafes under goat-hair tenting, its international restaurants and knick-knack stores that have provided a public square where native Qataris mix with foreigners, Suq Waqif was nominated for the Aga Khan Award.

The committee praised Suq Waqif as "a unique architectural revival of one of the most important heritage sites in Doha." They replaced "restoration" with "revival." Something intangible has been brought back: vitality, not material structures. Importantly, the committee describes the market as a city site, not a national site. In a speech thanking the Qatar ambassador in Paris for awarding him the Doha Capital of Culture Prize, the Aga Khan noted the emphasis on incorporating modern elements into the traditional architecture, on working "as forcefully on the making of Suq Waqif as it did on the construction of the modern Museum of Islamic Art. A wise policy achieved an exceptional success in combining modernity with authenticity or purity (*asala*) and in making them complement each other" (*Al-Raya*, November 15, 2010). Modernity and authenticity are paired as co-equals: both–and; neither–nor; and something else. *Barzakh* logic prevails in this tribal modern project. A powerful example of the "political and ideological charge of architecture in the service of nation building" (Bozdogan 2001, 294), this heritage project is designed for Qataris so that they can touch their past. But it is also for foreigners who can marvel at the resilience of a people able to survive where others could not.

CONCLUSION

Norman Foster's and Jean Nouvel's national museums, I. M. Pei's Museum of Islamic Art, and Muhammad 'Ali's Suq Waqif are part of the massive cultural makeover that Gulf Arab capitals are planning in their quest for "the Brand." Dozens more museums are in the planning stage.

Unlike Qatari Muhammad 'Ali's invention of vernacular architecture grounded in the tribal traditions of Gulf Arabs, French Jean Nouvel's project dives deep into the desert environment of the Bedouin and weaves it into the hypermodern of the twenty-first century Gulf. While Nouvel is explicit about foregrounding the desert and making it of a piece with the steel-glass modern, Muhammad 'Ali resists the skyscrapers. In a spring 2012 interview filmed in Mathaf, the museum of modern Arab art, he said, "Seeing those towers (skyscrapers) makes me feel I do not belong. They are not humane."[25] And yet they, too, are integral to what Qatar is becoming. Arguably, they are as essential to the national brand as are the national and Islamic museums and Suq Waqif; together they display the complementarity of the modern and the tribal. Moreover, these iconic parts of the city are connected and separated on Doha's Corniche. On one side of the bay are the low-lying themed museums, Suq Waqif and Mesheireb, a new neighborhood to be built in accordance with vernacular traditions; and on the other side loom the skyscrapers. On the left is the past and on the right the future. Past and future are being simultaneously constructed, while between them is the *barzakh* of the present that most Qataris, and especially the young, negotiate daily.

In the next chapter, I look at the ways in which states are adapting the tribal modern brand into heritage sites. They are inventing new versions of tribal sports and using the brand to revise undesirable elements from the past.

CHAPTER SIX

Heritage Engineering

Everyone loved this small, quaint town, and every guest from across the seas was amazed by its people who had lived here for centuries. It was a calm and peaceful land where you could hear the murmur of the sea and birds singing. The air was clean and full of happiness. Even when you were sick, this land would bring life to your body, cleansing all your organs. People were kind and generous. Although they were poor, and did not have enough food for their daily meals, they offered any guest who visited them hospitality that he would never forget. What is this land I am talking about? Who are these people? It is Al Shamal, the original home of most tribes of Qatar, including my tribe Al Kubaisi. This town, about 100 kilometers north of Doha, was also home to many other tribes: Al Mannai, Al Naimi, Al Kuwari, Al Kaabi, and Al Mohunadi. These tribes were like one hand; they worked together, and, most importantly, they were friends in war. Now all my tribe members in Doha have left their original home, leaving behind all those good memories...You see, Shaikh Khalifa Bin Hamad Al Thani, our ruler in that era, approved an order for all tribes in Al Shamal town to come to Doha. The first tribe that agreed was ours ... In the end, 'No history, no present' is a traditional saying of our grandfathers that indicates the importance of family history.   Al Kubaisi 2010, 43, 45

This narrative by a young Qatari man tells the story of his family's move from their original home to Doha. It is a move from tribal harmony in a coastal town to the impersonal fragmentation of city life. In those days, tribes lived like the fingers of one hand. Outsiders appeared only briefly and occasionally, and hospitality to strangers was an unquestioned protocol. Memories bind the wounds of loss and weave wonderful stories on the loom of nostalgia.

MODERNIZING DIFFERENTLY

The Arab Gulf states, whose citizens are the first generation to grow up with a national rather than a regional and primarily tribal identity, now want to write a largely unrecorded history. This longed-for past lies beneath the surface of nearly identical, newly global cities. Foremost in this construction of new pasts is what Amy Mills calls "nostalgic gentrification" (Mills 2008, 387). Investors are venturing into neighborhoods abandoned during the 1960s when they were considered backward and an obstacle to modernization. Now, however, with value inhering in the past, in the tribal, recent large-scale heritage projects demonstrate patriotism. For Ibrahim Jaidah and Malika Bourennane, their research into vernacular Qatari architecture has made "an exemplary patriotic contribution by exploring, researching and creating a unique history based on our own experiences and practices for future generations to remember" (Jaidah and Bourennane 2009, 10).

During the past decade, urban heritage projects have become a national priority for all Gulf countries.[1] In Bahrain, the Minister of Culture Shaikha May Al Khalifa designed the Shaikh Ebrahim Bin Muhammad Al Khalifa Centre for Cultures in Muharraq, the former capital of the island-state and the heart of a revitalized Bahraini culture. Galleries of traditional crafts like *kurar*, or gold embroidery, of contemporary art, and a poetry center draw people into the downtown their grandparents had fled. The mansion of Shaikh Matar, a Saudi pearl merchant who settled in Muharraq at the turn of the twentieth century, has been turned into a museum. It marks the beginning of the Pearl Road project that UNESCO designated in 2010 as a World Heritage site to honor Bahrain's central role in 6,000 years of pearling, the oldest extant historical activity in the larger Middle East.

Each state in the UAE has some form of state-sponsored heritage project. Sharjah's Heritage Directorate has restored an entire neighborhood in the downtown area, including the Sharjah fort and Bait al-Nabouda, the nineteenth-century house of a pearl merchant. They are part of a wider revitalization project that the Sharjah Emir Shaikh Sultan bin Muhammad Al Qassimi is sponsoring. Ras al-Khayma's Documentation and Studies Center focuses on local heritage and history. In Dubai, Iranians reclaimed the Bastakia neighborhood from local South Asians and turned it into a pedestrian area replete with high, windowless walls and wind towers, atmospheric cafes, two boutique hotels, and a museum that takes the visitor through 5,000 years of history undergirding one of the world's showiest cities. The name Bastakia reveals its *ajami* or Persian roots; its early inhabitants came from the Bastak region in Iran where thirteenth-century Arabs had fled from the Mongol hordes descending on Baghdad.

This is how the "creative industries" function. In the newly gentrified districts of Gulf cities, entrepreneurs open ethnographic museums with dioramas depicting the romance sans hardship of the desert and the pearl diving of the past. Art galleries and studios entice artists into formerly abandoned sites. Galleries become a magnet for visitors who need restaurants and cafes if they are to linger and buy. The liveliness of these art neighborhoods attracts commercial and residential real-estate developers with grandiose plans for luxury apartment blocks. Five-star hotels follow suit. Doha's Sharq Village and Spa, along with Dubai's One and Only Royal Mirage, are copies of American copies of an imagined Middle Eastern original. These hotels are created in the image of an Orient seen through the eyes of the West, for the West. Facilities are being constructed to welcome all who wish to partake of the exotic hedonism of a tribal modern universe.

Global villages like the Dubai Heritage Village and Qatar's Katara Cultural Village opened in 1997 and 2010, respectively. In both cases, the sites mix heritage projects with ultramodern facilities. Katara's marble amphitheater with its high-tech sound system evokes a Roman past that never was. Producing the past as a plastic pastiche of orientalist fantasies for an increasingly demanding cultural tourism industry, such heritage projects promote local traditions and culture for a new generation of Gulf Arabs out of touch with their own relatively recent past (Bristol-

Rhys 2011, 25). These heritage projects aim to restore the kind of vibrant, indigenous past that promises a cosmopolitan future.

To retrieve such a past, these sites eliminate undesirable elements like abject poverty, on the one hand, and millennia of trading contacts on the other. Stories of isolation erase the history of mutual cultural influences so that the multicultural distills into a local DNA. The dialectic of the pure and the multicultural is shaping the history of the region.

HERITAGE SPORTS

The culture industry is busy crafting new memories to be housed in national or "living museums." These living museums feature intangible culture such as camel racing, falconry,[2] and pearl diving spectacles so that visitors can look in on the vestiges of what were imagined to be majestic tribal cultures. They provide the pageantry that lends depth and dignity to new petro-states. These heritage spectacles help to brand distinctive (if similar) national projects.

One of the major surprises for any student of the Arab Gulf is the mythology surrounding pearls and camels. Neither pearl diving nor camel racing as they are practiced today are ancient pursuits. Political anthropologist Sulayman Khalaf has explored what he calls the invention of both the pearl diving romance in Kuwait and of camel racing in the UAE. Every summer since 1986, the Kuwait Pearl Diving Academy has held an annual Pearl Diving Festival that Khalaf considers to be part of a system of living museums that "provide both cultural/symbolic material required for the making of a state ... [promoting] the popular perception of [leaders'] roles as both patrons-cum-guardians of national heritage as well as state modernisers" (Khalaf 2008, 40, 41). This kind of leadership is providing a model for today's multinational CEO.[3]

For twelve days, over one hundred Kuwaiti boys with their trainers reenact the ordeals of their grandfathers. State-orchestrated ceremonies inaugurate and close the pearling expedition that revives "for the modern nation the heritage of its ancestors" (59). The media, and especially television, cover the twelve days, focusing on the ceremonies and the national leaders who sponsor the sea heritage culture. The pearl diving festival maintains "the nation's sense of cultural authenticity (*asala*), celebrating the achievements of national leadership and safeguarding it against the global culture" (64). Heritage symbology undergirds modern political power. Pearl diving and dhow extravaganzas are also staged in other Gulf states. Qatar's 2011 dhow festival included a twenty-four-hour outing for young men intent on honing their diving skills. Picturesque pearling boats, beautifully restored and moored in highly visible places, provided the suitable décor. These festivals serve several functions: they spectacularize the power of the state; they acknowledge the crucial role of the leaders in preserving the past; and they highlight local modernization projects, seeming to say: Look, that's what we were and where we are now.

CAMEL RACING

The mediatization of heritage culture shapes the latest version of camel racing popular throughout the region. Khalaf has traced the changes in camel racing from a relatively short performance that celebrated weddings and circumcisions to today's drawn-out mechanized spectacle. Indeed, the mechanization of this heritage sport is total. It has five principal elements.

First, a car accompanies each camel on the road that lines the course, to monitor and control the camel's movement.

Second, robot jockeys since 2006 have replaced the child jockeys who had attracted negative international attention to the races.

Third, and ironically, the prize is a car, usually a Toyota truck, and it is said that the camel, referred to as she, "has won a car" (Khalaf 1999, 104). In other words, the tribal camel and the modern car are interchangeable in the heritage sports *barzakh*.

Fourth, television has "played a significant role in the evolution and popularization of this cultural sport. It has not only fashioned the nature and style of producing cultural messages related to camel racing, but has also shaped other supporting activities surrounding this sport" (89). The media broadcast the event to a local and international audience as an explicitly *national* performance often sponsored by rulers who are praised for their concern to revive "our authentic popular heritage ... our authentic Arab customs and traditions" (102).

Fifth, camel breeding and training has become a highly technical process. Like racehorses, camels are bred not for domestic need but for the races.

It is the race that marks the camel's new symbolic capital in these hypermodern tribal societies. Bearing little resemblance to their forerunners, these races have changed the camel's role in the life of the tribe. No longer an integral part of tribal life, providing transport, wool, milk, and meat, as well as occasional spectacles, today the camel lives sequestered from the daily life of the people. The races do not celebrate special occasions; they are their own events held in large stadiums whose ten-kilometer course can only be followed on screens placed opposite the stands. The display of tribal icons like tents, Bedouin outfits, and a camel market adjoining the stadium, all reference recognizable fragments of the tribal heritage. Together, however, they create a new activity as unrecognizable to the pre-oil Gulf Arab as is Suq Waqif to the 1950s customers of flour and wool.

An important feature of the races is poetry. Poets praise the camel and also the tribal shaikhs, including the national ruler, who may be in attendance. The poetry recitals in the Nabati, or Bedouin dialect, attenuate cognitive dissonance, for they have remained the truest to their pre-oil roots. Poetry is the art par excellence of the Bedouin, whose nomadic lifestyle did not allow for the transport of nonvital, material art objects. Yet, even camel racing poetry has changed. Whereas in the past, poets tailored their poems to specific and known audiences, today the recitals are widely broadcast to unknown viewers. They advertise and help to brand "cultural authenticity and identity of the modern nation-state ... The constituent qualities of a great leader appear in these poems and other media discourses to embody the essential virtues of traditional tribal leaders (courage, honor, chivalry, nobility, generosity, wisdom, and respect for traditions) and the vision of state modernizers" (Khalaf 2000, 255, 256). The great leader is at once the traditional tribal shaikh and also the master builder of the modern nation-state.

Not all appreciate these official poems. Kuwaiti Salem Sayar Mohsin Al Anzi, who works in the Ministry of Information, writes fearlessly about the artificiality of these events. He bemoans the regrettable poetry, especially when penned by the rich and powerful:

The rich don't know you exist
Nor do your princes.
They just hire you
To blister your hands,
Applauding and
Whistling appreciatively
For their poems at soirees.

Paine, Lodge, and Touati 2011, 119

PEARL DIVING

Memories of the pre-oil space now transformed into national, metropolitan places are fast fading. The grim reality of a poverty-stricken past has been replaced with a form of nostalgia for they know not quite what.

The nostalgia for a past full of pageantry erases memories of the harsh humdrumness and also dangers of existence in the desert and at sea. In Bahrain, soap operas with a pre-oil backdrop, what Clive Holes calls "nostalgia *musalsalat*," (Holes 2005, 66) have become popular. Simple plots that emphasize singing and dancing present the joy and community that have been lost: "life may have been hard, but the hardships were bearable because they were shared by all. This is the kind of soap that comes with a free pair of rose-tinted spectacles [that] presents a part of the image that those who control it wish to project to the outside world" (55, 71). The soaps remember the past as noble, warm, and welcoming; they evoke a sharp contrast with the cold and impersonal present.

In the excitement of reenactment, the brutality of the past is forgotten, or, rather, it has been deliberately erased. One of the most challenging aspects of that past was the pearl diving on which shaikhly economies depended. Today, the divers are romanticized and the dangers they faced minimized; yet some challenge the myth.

Over forty years ago, the dangers of pearl diving were vividly represented in Kuwaiti filmmaker Khalid Al Siddiq's *Bas ya bahr* (1971), translated into English as "The Cruel Sea. Kuwait before Oil." The first feature film made by the state of Kuwait, it was shot on site during the late 1960s when oil had already transformed Kuwait into a wealthy country. This story of a pearl diver going blind because of the sea salt, his arm paralyzed after a shark bit him, presents life in a destitute pre-oil Kuwait. The film is shot in two locations: an alley, flanked by high white walls, and the sea. The alley, empty except for the occasional passerby or donkey, is where the diver's son Musa`id courts Nura, the daughter of a pearl dealer, the elite of Kuwaiti society at the time. Coming from different classes, theirs was an impossible love. Yet, like Romeo and Juliet, they risk all to see each other. Through the barred window on the second floor of her home, Nura exchanges longing looks with Musa`id. Devastated by the cruelty of pearling, his father has forbidden him to dive. The young man rails against this prohibition, for pearl diving was the only way pre-oil Kuwaitis who were not merchants or dealers could earn a living at that time. If he does not dive, he will not be able to afford the wedding with the woman he craves. Like his parents, Nura resists his entreaties to join the divers.

"I'm afraid," she repeats again and again. "You love the sea more than me."

But he must dive to feel he is a man and to earn the where-withal with which to marry her. Those who stay at home, he protests, are not real men; they live "a life full of humiliation." Musa`id knows that he cannot marry Nura if he does not dive. Eventually, his father, called *shaikh al-ghasa* in honor of his twenty-year career as master diver, gives his permission. Overjoyed, Musa`id eagerly accepts his father's equipment. When the time comes for the departure, his parents accompany him to the shore and watch him climb into the pearling boat that will take him and his fellow divers out to sea. The sound of their dirge-like chanting deepens the sense of dread hanging over the father and mother sitting helpless on the sand.

"Oh sea," the old diver wails, "you paralyzed me, and today I've handed you my son." Locked in her room, Nura, too, hears the divers' melancholy chant.

Meanwhile, Musa`id pegs the divers' clip of tortoise shell to his nose, hangs the oyster basket around his neck, and jumps overboard. Flashbacks to his father keep us under water, breathlessly watching the two of them for endless minutes as they scavenge for oysters from the seabed. At this point in the film, the scenes lengthen to hand the role of hero over to the suffering bodies. During the dive we hear the regular beat of a drum, of the men's hearts accompanying their urgent search.

Back on land, Nura's father contemptuously refuses Musa`id's father's request that they give their children to each other. Realizing that the boy and girl must have met unofficially and against the norms of the society, he beats Nura for long, painful minutes before announcing that he has arranged for her immediate marriage to an old merchant, aptly named Saqr, or falcon. The wedding scene drags on and on into the night, ending with a brutal rape. The camera rests cruelly on the bloodstained sheet.

The four months of the pearling season are finally over and the divers prepare to return to Kuwait. Musa'id dives one last time, perhaps to prove his manliness and certainly in the hope of finding the perfect pearl that will seal his fortune. Lack of experience spells his downfall; he reaches inside a huge open clam that clamps down on his hand. In his panic, Musa'id tears off his nose clip and, to the sound of the drumbeat, he swallows the salt water that drowns him. The divers retrieve the body, ritually wash it, wrap it in a shroud, then pray over it and slip it overboard. They have done this before.[4]

Although *Cruel Sea* does not spend much time with the captain, it is clear that he is a harsh master to be feared and slavishly obeyed. This image of the heartless creditor pervades literature on pearl diving. Emirati Ali Abdul Aziz al-Sharhan and Salma Matar Sayf have written of these captains' cruelty. Al-Sharhan's short story about a former pearl diver does not compromise in detailing the toll that work exacted. Addressing God, he exclaims: "you took all the days of my youth and squandered them on pearl diving at sea [...] we suffered such distress, fatigue, and grief, days when one didn't taste any rest or happiness. We would spend four months at sea, diving in the dark shallows, in search of a mere morsel of bread and enduring curses and abuse from the ship's captain [...] how many men perished in its waters, and how many men became slaves to debt?" (Johnson-Davies 2009, 20–21). In "The Hymn," Salma Matar Sayf writes of a man with "the heart of a skipper of one of those pearl-diving ships; he cold-heartedly buries his dead sailors by tossing them overboard" (Jayyusi 2005, 660). The cruelty of these sea captains who held their divers in debt slavery has become legendary. No rest for the divers; no happiness; only distress, fatigue, and grief. This was the grueling life of most Gulf Arab men in the pre-oil days. Neither the film nor the stories betray a hint of the glamour now embroidering the images of the diving past.

Poets also have stripped that past of romanticism. Kuwaiti poet Shurooq Amin is scathing:

> Sea-sticky
> like palm-leaf
> matting, brown-
> leather skin
> thin from years
> of diving,
> breath borrowed
> by waves that
> slurp the shore,
> tell me, son,
> as you lie
> heartbeat-less
> on my deck
> how to spare
> your mother
> these tidings.
>
> Paine, Lodge, and Touati 2011, 124

Amin links the young man's corpse to the mother's grief. Her poignant desperation is echoed in Emirati poet Maisoon Al-Qasimi's description of the pearl slipping out of the oyster shell "into your depths/ beside his drowned corpse/ that still clutched/ the empty oyster" (Paine, Lodge, and Touati 2011, 333). The empty oyster shell mirrors the tragic life of men doomed to die in the dive. These women poets harbor no illusions about the unrelenting brutality of the pre-oil world.

NOSTALGIA FOR THE SIMULACRUM

"Nostalgia is a kind of currency: the more it circulates the greater the power for creating common bonds, perceptions and imagining. It is a significant component in invoking collective historical memory" (Khalaf 2008, 66). Erasing pre-national hybrid ethnoscapes, nostalgia helps to construct the tribal modern and to provide the tabula rasa on which the mass migrations can be projected as new. The country becomes unprecedentedly international, but also, importantly, at ease in its new cosmopolitanism.

This nostalgic discourse creates a past worth saving and restoring. The harshness of survival in the desert, the cruelty of pearl diving that left young men weak, blind, and deaf, and the dangers of piracy and continuous warfare are all erased and replaced with attractive art and word images.

Instead, some writers project the life and values of the noble Bedouin as the panacea to counteract the threats of oil wealth that have flung them into global modernity. In "My Body is a Palm Tree that Grows on Bahr al-Arab," Kuwaiti princess Suad Al Mubarak Al Sabah (b. 1942) composes an elegy to the time of the pearl—minus the diver. She weeps for the loss of a pre-oil, prelapsarian world:

> I am the daughter of Kuwait
> I grew up with the pearls of the sea
> And nestled in my lap the shells and the stars
> The sea was kind to me, and Oh! So liberal!
> Then came the damned devil of oil
> And all fell prostrate at his feet
> And worshipped night and day
> We forgot the desert ethics, its honor and hospitality

Figure 12. Doha Corniche tile mural depicting a pearl diver.

Our coffee mortars, our ancient poetry
And drowned in trivialities
And all that was bright, real and great
Was swept away...
Then came the curse of oil,
And what was forbidden became common practice.
Our orchards became hot beds of sin,
And the cheap perfume of foreign adventuresses
Filled the night air...
Rise up in anger!
For gold has made you drunk,
And vanity made you blind.
I won't believe that oil is a fate we can't escape...
I shall always keep on waiting
For the flowers that will sprout
Under all these ruins.

Paine, Lodge, and Touati 2011, 91–95

Gold, black gold has made them all drunk. Those pearls of the past are not in the hands of a desperate young man, saltwater-wet with blood trickling out of his ears. The slime of the oyster host is gone; all that remains is the iridescent luster of the jewel on the neck of a princess. Suad Al Sabah lauds a kind, liberal sea, yet it took the sight and hearing of countless young men. She curses the black gold, yet it created the possibility for Gulf states to become players on the world stage. Hers is a call to resist, to rage against the oil that has erased the timeless values of the desert, erased the poetry that is her lifeblood, her instrument of resistance against the trivialities of this new world of empty luxury where the forbidden is permitted; drunkenness is the norm; and all is vanity.

Although she was the director of the Kuwait stock exchange, Al Sabah does not hesitate to denounce it and its values that have turned Arabs away from their duty and responsibilities to fellow Arabs:

My country
Put down the currencies bulletin, leave the stock exchange
And join the Arab forces

The obsession with wealth has ruined her homeland that is "Racked by oppression and suppression" (Paine, Lodge, and Touati 2011, 93–94). The damned devil of oil haunts her writing, even though she tries to believe that its curse can be escaped, that she has "escaped the contamination of the age of oil" (91).[5] However hard it may be, she is determined to continue her search for the flowers, the eternally beautiful but also unreal symbols of the pre-oil world, hoping against hope that they may yet bloom from under the debris of her land's ruins.

This elegy for a paradise lost recalls the writings of westerners in thrall of the desert exotic and the canvases of orientalist painters like Eugene Delacroix and Jean Léon Gérôme that are proudly displayed in local museums. Sharjah's national museum has devoted six of its eight galleries to orientalist art, and in Doha the Orientalist Museum will open in 2015 with paintings that Shaikh Hasan Al Thani, the cousin of the former Emir of Qatar, has collected from international auction houses. Celebrated locally as true, almost photographic depictions of life in the nineteenth century, these paintings are considered to be invaluable archives of Arabian life: "'I recognize this life,' Sheik Hassan said. 'The sheik sitting in his tent, I know these costumes are 100 percent right—even the tint of the button. The hare, it is from North Africa.' The paintings are not simply relics of cultural imperialism, he added. 'You should think of all of this as art of a cultural movement, an exchange of ideas" (Ouroussoff 2010). But there seems to be less a cultural movement or exchange of ideas than a celebration of the outsiders' gaze at the tribal past.

The images below illustrate the striking correspondence between the orientalist fantasy and today's local reenactment. The first image, in the style of John Frederick Lewis, depicts an Arab master with his black slave, each riding on lavishly accoutered camels. The dust kicked up by the camel hooves indicates that they are moving fast enough to be in some kind of a race. Behind them, two Arabs on horseback converse despite the speed of their galloping mounts. Tents in the background with tethered horses suggest that people are assembling for a special occasion. The second image catches a moment in a contemporary camel race. In the background this time we see not tents but the trucks accompanying the race. The two images portray succinctly the metamorphosis of the camel in the life of the Arabs.

The traveler Wilfred Thesiger elegized the "disappearance from Arabia of the traditional Bedouin way of life, the result of the inevitable involvement of the Bedouin today with the materialistic civilization of the modern world" (Bailey 2002, vii).[6] Anthropologist and collector of Bedouin poetry from Sinai and the Negev, Clinton Bailey regrets the passing of "the last generation whose lives were formed within the context of traditional Bedouin culture . . . their nomadic antecedents in these deserts stretching back to biblical, and often pre-biblical, times" (xi, 428).[7] It is on this canvas of dunes and camels that heritage projects are painted.

Figure 13. Painting of camels in Doha's Orientalist Museum.

Figure 14. Camel race 2010 (photo by Jonathan Cross).

Nostalgia for the simulacrum—longing for a past that never was—projects a pristine past that corrects confusion. Qatari Noof Khalid Al Suwaidi trembles at the thought that "globalization and modernization may strip Qatar of its cultural identity and sense of individuality... Qatar has neglected its cultural initiative for the sake of globalization and economic welfare" (Al Suwaidi 2010, 121). In her lament for a lost identity, Al Suwaidi finds no comfort in the heritage projects that have been planned around the city. Like their Qatari and Kuwaiti cousins, Emiratis also long for that abstract past free of both pain and poverty. A Zayed University student neatly summed up the contradiction: "We love our heritage but we don't like to be reminded that we were poor!" (Bristol-Rhys 2011, 121).

THE HEART OF DOHA

A surprising site of nostalgia in Doha is a small museum floating on the edge of the Corniche near the Sheraton Hotel. Photographs, objects, and a large maquette document the development of Doha from a 1947 mud-brick town with a population of ten thousand to the Heart of Doha, the Msheireb project to be completed by 2020. The Heart of Doha will gentrify what is today a lively Asian neighborhood adjacent to Suq Waqif by constructing vernacular residential and commercial buildings and pedestrian areas.

In the entry hall to the museum, a tombstone by a fountain announces the *barzakh* theme that epitomizes the Msheireb mission: "A meeting, not a melting of cultures." On another wall, a video features Shaikha Mozah, consort of the former Emir, connecting modernity and authenticity through architecture: "We are trying to fill the void we have in our architecture…(The Msheireb project) is a cry to everyone to be involved in our architecture." The theme of the first gallery is "A Blueprint for the Future," and the visitor is asked: "Can we remain rooted to our values and our culture, and still embrace the modern world?" The answer to this Platonic question of course is yes. The visitor then steps back to Qatar's earliest history.

The first legend announces that Qatar's history began in "the Stone Age, 50,000 years ago. The wealth of rock carvings found at Jebal Al Jassariya (*sic*) offers evidence of an ancient cultural heritage." After several thousands of years, Herodotus mentioned Katara. Next, approximately twenty-three hundred years later, the visitor reads about William Palgrave. During his 1863 visit to Doha, Palgrave apparently said: "We welcomed the whole world in our country"—a celebration of early cosmopolitanism in striking contrast with his shocked descriptions of Doha's abject poverty, especially the Suq Waqif market. In the next gallery, Education City (an extravagant importation of American education to Doha) is praised for allowing youth to retain traditional values by studying in Qatar instead of traveling abroad for their education.

This story of a deep national history at ease with its modern, cosmopolitan, urban vision is overshadowed by a loud documentary that can be heard throughout the two galleries. The Arabic voiceover with English subtitles booms its lament for the past, a lost past that haunts the confusing present, represented by flashing images of traffic jams and mad mall scenes. In that idyllic past, we hear, people lived close to each other, knew each other intimately, and their homes were places of open hospitality.

An elderly man on the screen complains

Today, I am alone, I am looking for company. Today, people use cell phones to connect. We barely know each other. The world has changed. Doha was different; Doha has grown. We barely know each other. Today, all they [an accelerated image of young women and men streaming up and down mall escalators, cell phones glued to their ears, has just flashed on the screen] think of is work. We're comfortable but we long for the past that will not return. Oh, my God, in my solitary moments I dream of the past, when we were all one family. We need to learn about our past and pass it on to our children. Without a past there is no present. Those wonderful days will never return. Our glorious past is the heart of our modern world. Oh, Qatar my country, I long for the past.[8]

This dirge about isolation full of clichés about the lost past, in a context where Qataris have lost all human connections as they rush alone through throngs of foreigners, is unrelenting.

CONCLUSION

Qatari filmmaker Khalifa al-Muraikhi presents a similarly puzzling story of longing for the past and rejection of the highly touted present. *Watch Hands* is the first all-Qatari film. It came out in 2010 and narrates the vertiginous jump of Doha from a habitation for the hardy few to a global tourist, trade, and political hub. The focus is on an old man shuffling slowly along the Corniche and marveling at the Wall Street-like skyline. Turning inland, he walks toward Suq Waqif, where he watches tourists photograph the oddest objects.[9] They value the old, murmurs one of his friends, and we value the new. The old man sits down.

Pulling out a pocket watch, the time icon that recalls the rose in *Citizen Kane* and Proust's madeleine, the hero travels back in time. The watch hands hurtle backwards to his childhood and young adulthood in a mud-hut settlement filled with magic and jinn. His father had been one of the tribal leaders who practiced pagan rituals in the dark of night. The boy had watched in awe from afar. The film ends abruptly in modern Doha with the death of the old man. The transition between these two eras is erased. The old man cannot deal with the contradictions. The youth will have to forge an identity that takes the best from the past and the future.

Viewers of the film, like visitors to the Msheireb Museum, may also feel confused. How can the tribal modern project recall the past it is expected to deploy? An answer came the following year from the newly launched Doha Film Industry, the DFI.[10] The release of "Black Gold" (later released as "Day of the Falcon") erased the ambivalence about the past. Depicting the same pre-oil era as *Cruel Sea*, French director Jean-Jacques Annaud produced a Hollywoodesque fantasy. No more destitute pearl divers for him, but rather princes wearing bright white, gold-embroidered *thawbs*, falling in love with beautiful women. Like the Bedouin in Munif's *Cities of Salt*, they fight each other over the black gold that some Texans have just discovered, and the honor of staying true to the eternal norms and values of their tribes. Epic scenes of battles played out against the pure emptiness of the desert alternate with lush *1001 Nights* vignettes recalling a time of luxury. The film's director is French, and the actors, including Antonio Banderas, Freida Pinto, and Mark Strong, are mostly non-Arabs playing the parts of Arabs. According to one critic, the film recalls "Hollywood super-productions of the 50s or 60s."[11] Here again we see the copy of the copy without an original, or the image that shapes the brand. This brand, that picks the best from the past and preserves it for the future, shapes performances of national identity.

CHAPTER SEVEN

Performing National Identity

When I look for my real self and can't find it, I say that it is lost in the terrors of a life where I am no longer myself. I have allowed the waves to toss my self to the right and to the left. Although I am in it, life has distanced me from my self... When I wear my *thawb* [white gown], and *gutra* and walk on the earth of which I am a part... the pebbles delight in my walking and they sing: Oh Arab! And the air of the earth embraces me and takes from my scent to spread it among the passersby. Every day I go to my friend the Stone and she knows me by my *thawb*, *gutra* and `*uqal* [headdress] and my perfume and I tell her all my secrets and we have become friends. One day, I changed clothes and left my *thawb*, *gutra* and `*uqal* at home and I sat on the Stone and she said: Who are you? And I said: I'm your friend who sits with you every day. She said: You're not my friend because your appearance and your *thawb* and your smell are not the same. And the Stone pushed me away violently and I fell into a lions' den and they tore my body to pieces, some from the West, some from the East and some from I don't know where. As I was drowning among my severed limbs, I heard a voice calling me. I looked up quickly and heard my *thawb*, *gutra* and `*uqal* saying, Come to us for

we are your saviors, your features. If you abandon us you will
be lost without identity and no one will know who you are.

This fairy tale by 'Abd al-Karim al-'Izzazi appeared in the
Qatari daily *Al-Raya* on September 7, 2010, three days before the
end of Ramadan. It narrates the important role national dress
plays in marking Gulf Arabs' national difference, authenticity,
and identity. Gulf Arabs are increasingly donning a uniform that
turns every public appearance into a performance of national
identity.[1] Men's *thawb*, *gutra*, and *'uqal* and women's *'abaya* have
become more than everyday formal dress, they are the *sine qua
non* of national performances (Longva 1997, 116–25).

Local dress signals not only the nationality but also the privileged status of Gulf and Peninsula Arabs. It marks their difference from outsiders. In the second volume of 'Abd al-Rahman
Munif's *Cities of Salt*, we read the consternation of tribal men
when they see an outsider wear their dress. On his way back
from the Hajj, a Syrian doctor establishes a clinic in Harran
where he dispenses miracles. Despite his white skin and elegant
western clothes marking him as the outsider par excellence, Dr.
Mahmalji ingratiates himself with the Emir. The people not
only accept him, they come to believe in him (Munif 1989, 520–
35). After caring for the dying ruler and cozying up to his son,
the new ruler, the doctor appears in the town wearing a *thawb*:
"He had discarded the foreign clothes that used to distinguish
him from those around him and had adopted wide, flowing Arab
dress in which he drowned. He did not know how to wear it prop-
erly and while he walked he kept tripping over himself" (Munif
1986, 10). But, not for long. He soon learned how to walk in these
new clothes as though he were one of them. At first the people

did not recognize him, but when they did, they became alarmed at how quickly this stranger had become comfortable in their clothes. The disguise singled him out as someone to fear. He, like all foreigners adopting Gulf Arab clothes, must be closely watched. He must have an ulterior motive for going native.

An Emirati woman student I met in Abu Dhabi told me that restricting native dress to Gulf Arabs is a survival mechanism in "countries where the local population is the minority."[2] Rejecting anonymity in the crowds of foreigners, Gulf Arabs perform nationality and privilege through tribal dress. Men's national dress has become a sign of "cultural authenticity and connectedness to past traditions. Without hesitation Emiratis will say that the *kandoura* is the dress of their ancestors and they remain loyal to it, 'our dress is our identity.'" Displaying authenticity, wealth, power and privilege, clothes "have become markers of a dominant ethnic class presiding over the affairs of a multi-ethnic society in transition ... current adherence to their traditional national dress is a function of both tradition and modernity; modernity in the sense that it is a reaction or protest to threatening global forces" (Khalaf 2005, 244–45). While the form of this national dress is said to be traditional, its meaning is modern inasmuch as it affirms a new national identity in the twenty-first century. For some, national dress also represents a protest against globalization, the flattening effects of jeans for everyone.

Denoting a collective construction of social boundaries, national dress is not a throwback but rather a conscious forward-looking reaction to the conditions of daily life. In fact, Bristol-Rhys contests the assumption that national dress is traditional. Citing some older women she interviewed, she observes,

There was no possible way that a white *kandoura* would have been worn regularly before there was running water, washing machines, irons, starch and, to be honest, maids. A glimpse at any of the pictures taken of people before the late 1960s shows men dressed in various shades of brown and black, and not white. Only the rulers seemed to have managed white with any frequency. The `abaya* was worn in the pre-oil days but, as one woman pointed out, you were never really in the 'public view' in the settlements and towns so it did not have to be worn all the time. 'It isn't national dress any more, it's the national uniform,' laughs Masifa. 'It is the only way to be recognized as citizens' (Bristol-Rhys 2011, 112).

This national uniform, Longva suggests, may be state-authorized. Unlike the assumption that the *thawb* and the `abaya* were naturally and almost unthinkingly adopted by people under threat of disappearance, she claims that it is "a result of an ideological mobilization under the aegis of the state: the formation of a national identity" (Longva 1997, 125). The *thawb* and the `abaya* have become vivid icons of a newly embraced, exclusivist, elitist national identity, and as such this national uniform is out of bounds for foreigners. *Gulf News* reported on September 15, 1996, Emiratis' concern about non-nationals wearing their clothes "so that they could pass off as nationals, hoping that they would get preferential treatment" (Khalaf 2005, 263).

The nationalist aspect may be as blatant as adorning `abayas* "with portraits of Sheikh Muhammad al-Maktoum and Sheikh Maktoum al-Maktoum, the current and former rulers of Dubai, along with a map of the United Arab Emirates and the colors of its flag [ ... ] these `abayas* present a reification of national symbols" (Al Qasimi 2010, 69). The display of a modern, national subjectivity through dress "may be as old as human society ... the mod-

ern self may be less a matter of the content of an individual subjectivity than that of the insertion of that subjectivity into a
particular regime of historicity and sociopolitical management"
(Trouillot 2002, 853). In Jordan, for example, tribal dress differentiates Jordanians from the Palestinian refugees who migrated en
masse after two wars with Israel in 1948 and 1967.[3]

TRIBAL DRESS IN GULF HISTORY

During the 1960s and 1970s when tribes were being disaggregated,
western clothes performed modernity. Traditional dress became
almost taboo because it emphasized connection to the past and
thus impeded modernization. Today it is western dress that is
virtually taboo for Gulf Arabs, at least when they are at home.
According to Marxist theorist Fredric Jameson, the quintessential modern gesture is taboo: "what look like innovations are in
the modern, the result of a desperate attempt to find substitutes
for what has been tabooed. It is a model and a restructuration
that shifts the burden of proof from the future to the past…
the taboo is very explicitly a taboo on previous kinds of repre-
sentational form and content" (Jameson 2002, 127). In the mid-
twentieth-century Arab Gulf, the tribal was taboo; individual
and collective modernization/westernization was the mandate.

Replacing the tie and suit in the twenty-first century, "tribal"
dress is modern, national but, above all, it is also patriotic, as the
founder and owner of "Al-Motahajiba" told his daughter, a student of mine in the VCUQ class. Today, one of the largest `abaya*
franchises in the region with its own international fashion shows
(Al Qasimi 2010), "Al-Motahajiba" began modestly. Mr. Al Emadi

had launched his business in a nine-square-meter location in the old commercial district that Muhammad ʿAli ʿAbdullah's Suq Waqif replaced.

"The preservation of our culture and traditions started for me as a summer project in the year 1983 but it is now my mission against the winds of change blowing through our region. How to maintain your fashion edge against western trendy designers? . . . Our notion is as Henry Ford once noted: If your attention is focused on what you give for a dollar worth of sales rather than what you get, your business is bound to succeed. 'Al-Motahajiba' is a brand that we intend to preserve for centuries to come hoping to be a small contributor in a sacred cause, our culture."[4] Al Emadi's brother added that Al-Motahajiba "is the most famous and glamorous brand name in the fashion design sphere among Arab women." Note the use of the words "brand" and "sacred." Like Jaidah and Bourennane's attribution of patriotism to their research into vernacular architecture, Al Emadi believes his ʿabaya franchise has made a patriotic contribution to indigenous culture, and the culture he is referencing is not religious but national. At the same time, in its scope and intent it exceeds national boundaries. As Al Emadi's daughter Sara commented, "Al-Motahajiba may seem to be a brand, which grew from a small shop in the souq, but in reality it is a tribal network spanning borders and cultures."[5]

The connection between tribal dress, modernity, and patriotism is widespread. A respondent to the survey that my VCUQ students designed about the wearing of the *thawb* or the ʿabaya wrote: "I am comfortable wearing the ʿabaya wherever I travel and that is my choice. Often I am asked about it and my identity and I feel as though I am an ambassador for my country." When

I spoke with an Egyptian friend about this glorification of the `abaya she was amazed. She had always thought, she told me, that these super-rich women looked shabby in their black wraps. Clearly Gulf Arab women disagree. Far from shabby, tribal dress as national brand marks aristocracy. It distinguishes citizens from non-citizens, but it is also for international consumption.

Whereas Gulf men wear similar white gowns that are nonetheless nationally recognizable by collar or sleeve detail, women's black `abayas are not nation-specific. Fashions are often set in Saudi Arabia and then spread throughout the Peninsula where the `abaya plays not only a political but also a socio-economic role. Sulayman Khalaf writes, "The `abaya, when viewed within the Emirati elaborate system of ethnic stratification, becomes invested in multiple ways with social and cultural attitudes, meanings, images and symbols that help in the construction of the Emirati identity. The black `abaya has become the symbolic protected space for the Emirati woman, her spatial bubble, as it were, that not only protects but also differentiates and identifies" (Khalaf 2005, 242).[6] Men's dress code represents the national identity of individual states, while women's fashions are linked to the region as a whole.

A remarkable example of tribal dress as national icon was designed into one of Dubai's most iconic buildings: the 2007 Burj al-Arab that most believe is shaped like a dhow sail. The developers modeled this building on "a figure fitted with a *kandura* (long robe-like garment), *gutra* (headscarf), and *egal* (rope used to tie the *gutra* in place)" (Mitchell 2007, 136). Tribal dress, however stylized in architecture, makes a modern and immediately political statement.[7] Writing about Emirati dress "and the dynamics associated with its discourses," Khalaf confirms, "there are in our contemporary world different versions of modernity and different paths to it" (Khalaf 2005, 235).

While dress is one way of noting the mutually reinforcing overlap of the tribal modern, still another is Bedouin poetry.

THE MILLION'S POET

One of the most visible performances of the tribal modern is *Sha`ir al-Milyun*, or the Million's Poet competition. A reality TV competition, it assembles 18- to 45-year-old poets skilled in composing Nabati poetry, the colloquial poetics of the desert Bedouins, known for its improvisational spontaneity. The show has become very popular throughout the Arab world.[8]

Nabati poetry has always been an important part of tribal life; it was "the pinnacle of their aesthetic, creative ability, as an aesthetic relief from the starkness of the desert…They were also clearly proud to hear aspects of their culture elevated into verse… Bedouin poetry, like Bedouin culture, is heir to a Middle Eastern desert tradition that goes back four thousand years" (Bailey 2002, xii, 7, 15). Love of poetry is not new, but what is new is the interest in a poetic language that until recently Generation Twitter considered old-fashioned and taboo in the sense that it was connected to a past irrelevant to people intent on moving forward.

The brainchild of the crown prince of Abu Dhabi Shaikh Muhammad Bin Zayid Al Nahayan, the Million's Poet is a television talent show that the Abu Dhabi Authority of Culture and Heritage launched in November 2006. Performing the mutually constitutive tribal and modern in language, forty-eight contestants try to dazzle the jury that will honor the one who displays the greatest facility with the tribal language and millennial poetic conventions. Bedouin tribal poetry, with its obsolescing vocabulary, has stepped into the limelight. The winner, usually a man in his thirties, is awarded 1,000,000 Dinars and the title of the Million's Poet.[9] This is not an old-fashioned recital for elders. Young, hip Gulf Arabs attend this wildly popular competition in rhetorical tribal extravagance.

So popular has the show become among young people that some call it the Gulf Idol of poetry, à la American Idol. Poets stride on stage with music blaring, audience screaming, and lights flashing. They declaim their lines bombastically and then exit with equal pomp. Winners become national icons.

For a sense of the spectacle and also its incongruence a year into the Arab Spring, read this February 28, 2012, description of the fifth competition by Hugh Miles for the BBC News Middle East:

> The show is filmed live on Tuesday evenings in the Rafha Beach theatre, a heavily illuminated edifice in the desert on the road to Dubai. Inside, on the highly polished black stage bathed in gently shifting coloured lights, is what looks like a huge revolving flower with an oversized video screen at its centre. The auditorium is nearly full with a neatly self-segregated audience of men on one side, wearing traditional white dishdashas, and veiled women on the other in black abayas. Incense hangs pleasantly in the air, as from my seat behind the gold VIP tables I watch a qahwaji, a traditional coffee maker, serve the three judges Arabian coffee from a large ornamental brass pot...All the poetry is proudly Arab, Islamic and tribal, and none of it expresses the slightest desire for either westernisation or democracy.[10]

Beyond pure entertainment, this competition integrates the language and lyrics of the Bedouin elders into the high-tech media world, and in so doing it bolsters the power of tribal leaders and their new nations.[11] The competition trumpets the coveted tribal modern brand. In April 2012, Shaikh Muhammad Bin Zayid Al Nahayan, Crown Prince of Abu Dhabi and Deputy Supreme Commander of the UAE Armed Forces, attended the finals, and Rashid Ahmed Al Rumaithi became the first Emirati poet to win first prize.

The selection process is quite elaborate. Every November, the jury of Gulf poets and literary critics selects forty-eight Nabati poets from several different Arab countries, including the desert regions of Jordan, Syria, Iraq, and Libya. In December, they gather at the al-Raha Beach Hotel Theater in Abu Dhabi to begin the six-week television knockout contest. Chosen poets are given a week to compose a poem on a given subject. The jury's verdict is worth 30 percent, while the remaining 70 percent depends on public votes.

It is important to note that, like other heritage projects, this competition has a commercial, and political, aspect. Every person who calls in her vote knows that she will have the equivalent of a dollar deducted from her phone bill. The more calls, the happier the telephone company. It has been rumored that big donors have bought thousands of calls. Like camel racing, a tribal poetry performance is thus underwritten by twenty-first-century capital and technology.

During the first year, one of the several subjects imposed on contestants was "Loyalty to the Homeland." The winner of that 2006 competition was Qatari Muhammad bin Futas of the Al Murrah tribe. Like all competitors, he first proclaimed his identity to be national, and then tribal: "Qatar is my homeland and I am like any other person who grew up in it, the cameleer, the shepherd, the rich, the pearl diver and the farmer...Men in danger respond as a man willing to sacrifice their pride [the word used was *gutra*] and lives to save their country's dignity and glory." Again, a tribal heritage project links to nationality, and national pride is symbolized by the men's traditional headdress, the *gutra*.[12]

The next year's winner was also a Qatari, but Qatari with a twist. Khalil Al Shibrimi Al Tamimi was in fact a Saudi with a recently acquired Qatari citizenship. A member of the legendary Al Tamim tribe, he asserted kinship with the ruling Al Thanis, who also claim descent from the Al Tamim. He asked to be brought back into the bosom of the tribe. His wish was granted, and he brought home the coveted prize.

On October 18, 2011, "Middle East Online" reported that Saudi, Kuwaiti, Qatari, Moroccan, Iraqi, Yemeni, and Egyptian poets, some of them women, had come to Amman to audition: "Some of them defied all circumstances experienced by their countries and traveled thousands of kilometers to attend the event. One Libyan poet took a huge risk, traveling through the dangerous roads from the violence-torn Libyan capital and then by air to make it to Jordan. Many Yemeni poets also braved the ongoing unrest in their country as well as poets from Iraq, Syria and Palestine to meet the jury."[13] With the eyes of the world on the revolutionaries overthrowing their ensconced dictators, intrepid poets from Libya and Yemen were undeterred.

NEO-BEDOUIN LANGUAGE

The competition is flourishing. A grassroots version of the Million's Poet was exported to the Yemeni archipelago of Socotro:

"a geographically diverse body of contestants; a seated jury of experts; an audience seated on the ground of the Hadiboh public schoolyard; a grand prize of 100,000 Yemeni riyals ($450); and a glass trophy."[14] During the Yemeni uprising of 2011, contestants used the competition to air grievances against President ʿAli ʿAbdallah Salih.

Filmmakers and writers have created stories about Nabati poetry and the competition. In the early 1990s, Dubai short story writer Muhammad al-Murr wrote about a young man who hoped to inherit his uncle's talent for Nabati poetry. A television program about Nabati poets inspired him, and he composed a poem he had penned by a skilled calligrapher and sent it to a local paper. Three weeks later, the editor printed a dismissal of the poem as "feeble in content and flawed in its metre. It is a long way from Nabati poetry but we would like to praise you for your beautiful handwriting" (al-Murr 1991, 70). Tribal poetry has strict rules; only skilled poets should dare compose it. In 2012, the Abu Dhabi company Imagenation released "Million's Poet," a film about Salamah, a Bedouin girl who defied her father's prohibition on her participation in the Million's Poet competition.[15]

It is remarkable how popular the language of this wildly popular poetic endurance contest has become.[16] The revival of the Bedouin Nabati language coincides with a linguistic crisis among young Gulf Arabs. A Qatari student once confided that her English was better than her Arabic and her English was not native. She was ashamed, she said, that she had not mastered any language.[17] Dana Abdulla Al Khalaf echoes this sentiment: "In the past, the dialect in Qatar was a pure local Arabic, Khaliji [Arab Gulf] dialect, but it kept changing ... some of the causes of change in our dialect are the languages we learn in school,

multiculturalism, mass media, trade with different countries…
and globalization… most young people now don't even understand words our grandparents used" (Al Khalaf 2010).

The words their grandparents used now pepper the language
of the Million's Poet aspirants. Newspapers "carry weekly sections exclusively dedicated to *Nabati* poetry, and more than five
hundred Internet sites and blogs publish, discuss and circulate
Bedouin poems. These sites are growing by the day, along with
satellite programs and poetry contests… this genre is treated as
an object for consumption and fetishism in a rapidly and alarm-
ingly evolving consumer culture in the Gulf region" (al-Ghadeer
2009, 14). The celebration of Bedouin oral poetry challenges the
domination of English, but it also serves as a counterweight to
what many consider to be the diluted Arabic of the media, today's
lingua franca across the Arab world.

Conferences deplore the disappearance of formal Arabic.
During "The Arab Cultural Project" conference held in Doha,
November 12, 2010, linguist Faruq Shusha commented that young
people seem to think that their "modernity begins with a break
from their language." The mission of the Sharjah-based Arabic
Language Protection Association is the preservation of "the
Arabic language from an awkward mix of foreign vocabularies
and dialects, and to limit the negative influences of the multicultural environment on the UAE's official language… The
new generations are becoming more and more distant from their
native tongue. This has given rise to a new form of broken language that combines various accents emerging on the surface"
(Davidson 2008, 201, 202). The popularity of the Million's Poet
contest sparks the hope that Arabic in its unadulterated form may
yet return.

This search for the pure language of desert Bedouin recalls the role of eighth-century Basra in the formative period of Arabic philology and linguistics. Basra scholars "were not content to collect samples of speech from Bedouins from the desert, or Badiya, the steppes of Suria and Iraq, who came to their cities; they also took themselves into the desert to gather them from the mouths of other Bedouins, the authenticity of whose speech they judged to be intact because they had lived far from the centers of urban life... The beginning of the tenth century marked the emergence of a neo-Bedouinism that re-established a connection with the past of the Basra school by putting a stay in the desert on the agenda for scientific reasons" (Touati 2010, 51, 67). This tradition continued until the twentieth century, with "many urban families sending their children to live among the Bedouin for a few seasons in order to learn the lore of the Bedouin and to absorb the positive values of living in a simple society in the purity of the desert" (Cole 1975, 53). Now, Bedouin Arabic is being brought to the capital, even though some still believe that it is only by living among the Bedouin that they will be able to learn this language in its pure form.

In 2008, the Abu Dhabi Cultural Foundation, inspired by the success of the Million's Poet, opened the first Nabati poetry academy. According to its founder Mr. Amimi, "Nabati is not a new kind of art, but Million's Poet has brought it into more popular culture, not just here but across the region."[18] In fact, it is new. Like camel racing, Nabati poetry has been reintroduced in a way that looks quite different from its predecessor. Academy scholars travel throughout the region recording Bedouin poetry. In 2009, the Emir of Sharjah, Shaikh Sultan Bin Mohammad Al

Qasimi, opened the Sharjah Nabati Poetry Centre "built to serve present and future generations."[19]

Tribal dress and poetry are performing the brand in spectacular ways, and in the final chapter I will look at how women are engaging with the tribal modern brand as they become increasingly visible in the public sphere.

CHAPTER EIGHT

Gendering the Tribal Modern

I saw evil stalking from the eyes of their fatwas
In an era when they contaminated the permitted with the
    forbidden
I've uncovered the face of the truth
Revealing the monster hidden behind the mask
A savage, resentful, barbaric, blinded man
Wearing a cloak of death under a tightened belt
Howling and terrifying the populace through brutal politics
Preying on every soul yearning for peace
The voice of the truth seeks refuge, and rightness is dying in
    isolation
In the pursuit of self-interest the one who speaks freely is
    disgraced...

These are the words that Saudi journalist and mother of four Hissa Hilal dared to utter at the 2010 Million's Poet competition. She found the perfect platform to throw down the gauntlet. She was the first female finalist in the Million's Poet competition. Fully covered, she took her seat on the stage, faced the television

Figure 15. Hissa Hilal honored at the Million's Poet contest.

cameras and recited "The Chaos of Fatwas," her damning condemnation of religious men's misogynistic interpretations of Islam.

Echoing women poets like Suad Al Mubarak Al Sabah, who bemoaned an age when the forbidden is permitted and the permitted forbidden, Hissa Hilal attacked the religious authorities head on. They have become monsters wrapped in their cloaks of death. They howl and terrify the people and drive truth underground. Like vultures, they prey on peace-loving souls. They chase truth and freedom out of the public sphere.

There was an outcry in Saudi Arabia; people on several Islamic sites called for her head. Newspapers around the Arab world interpreted this unprecedented event to be a woman's declaration of war on evil fatwas. It was a daring but dangerous act. Hissa Hilal did not care, because the situation had become so intolerable for women that she had to protest. And in choosing to recite her poem in the most popular venue in today's Gulf region, she made sure that her protest would reach the widest audience possible.[1] Hissa Hilal didn't win, even though the judges scored her highly in every round. First and second places were assured by the people's vote, and so she finished in third place.[2]

On November 1, 2011, Hilal published an article in the Saudi English language newspaper *The National* entitled "A Particular Idea of Islam has come to dominate Society." She returned to the theme of Islamist arrogance, the proliferation of misogynist fatwas, and the attack on intellectuals and poets like her: "I'm a woman, and for an extremist there is no greater sin than a woman's embrace of literature and poetry." What greater compliment to the power of the word and of women than the fear of these religious zealots?

Gulf Arab women are taking up the challenge of modernity. Yet, they still have to grapple with the contradictions posed by life in the *barzakh* between tribal values and global norms. Some negotiate the *barzakh* with ease; others do not. Some write their anxiety quietly in the privacy of their homes, others shout their anger out loud.

UNEASY COSMOPOLITANISM AGAIN

"I don't care if the whole world knows! Yes, I do have a shrink."

Shrink. Such an odd word to tumble out of the mouth of a woman student I met in Abu Dhabi in December 2008.

"We don't know who we are. So, to make sure we're not confused with the foreigners we have to wear a uniform. We've lost our moorings."

The face to the world is awe-inspiring, but the inside story is something else. Young men and women born into the *Arabian*

Nights world of untold wealth and privilege are negotiating the contradictions between the tribal *thawb/dishdasha/kandura* and American jeans, between the `abaya and short skirts. Sons and daughters of illiterate parents have been catapulted into a new world of global business, culture, and politics. Skipping over the Gutenberg Revolution, they have jumped directly from orality to IT literacy, from the tribal to the modern, and in the process they have combined them.

Exciting? Yes! Terrifying? Yes and again yes!

Since the 1990s, women's participation "in the labor force more than doubled in Bahrain, Kuwait, Qatar and Saudi Arabia, while it almost tripled in Oman and the United Arab Emirates" (al-Kazi 2008, 172). More highly educated than the men, these young women are among the first generation to work outside the home, even if their numbers remain negligible.[3] Some, especially elite women, are enjoying and taking advantage of unprecedented freedoms. Others still have to contend with tribal values that emphasize domesticity and public invisibility that undermine the promise of education and independence.

Although they have scarcely begun to be politically active—Kuwaiti women achieved suffrage in 2005 and Saudi women in 2011 only—more women are entering decision-making positions. Issues of social and gender justice are more openly discussed today than even only a few years ago. Newly visible, women out in the public square provide the symbolic capital so important for new nations vying for global attention. Women in the workplace signal their nations' modernity; women in `abayas perform their countries' authenticity.

Two recent examples suggest the coming change in women's status. In August 2012, the Saudi government announced its intention to build a women-friendly industrial city in Hofuf, an oasis in the Eastern Province about 50 miles from the Gulf coast. Jobs in textiles, pharmaceuticals, and food-processing industries will employ about 6,000 women, thus boosting the government's Saudization goals. The Gulf countries are also concerned to lessen dependence on foreign workers.[4] In March 2013, hundreds of businesswomen from Gulf hydrocarbon producers met in London to discuss joint ventures with European counterparts. Such projects aim to expand regional women's role in the domestic economy.[5]

. . .

Some women are utterly at ease in the brand *barzakh*. This was evident at the December 2010 "Muslim Cosmopolitanism" conference Bruce Lawrence and I convened in the Doha Museum of Islamic Art. The Qatari women in my VCUQ class had organized a panel about the tribal in their everyday lives. Cutting-edge modern and a monument to the nation's religious and cultural heritage, the Museum of Islamic Art was the perfect place for what transpired. Reporting on their research, the students detailed young people's daily instinctive adjustments to non-stop change. Alertness to change and accommodation of the new, they agreed, did not compromise their commitment to the tribal. They were comfortable in both worlds, and at the same time critical of both. Dressed in Armani and Christian Dior jeans and Jimmy Choo and Gucci stilettos clearly visible under their half-open latest model `*abayas*, they performed cosmopolitan lives rooted in their millennial culture.

Foreigners in the audience were nonplussed: "Don't you feel torn between your grandparents' tents and those skyscrapers?"

One participant asked, gesturing out the window and across the bay.

"Not at all," they replied almost in unison and laughed.

Like them, the heroine of a story by Qatari Fatma Nasser Al Dosari "could not be happier" to be born into this time and place of privilege where women are treated "like queens." Traditions, she writes, "keep me secure ... they do not contradict with modernism; they both add value to your uniqueness and shape your identity" (Henderson and Rajakumar 2010, 82–85). Far from presenting these women with a problem, much less a crisis, the intermingling of the modern and the tribal is pleasurable.

In her analysis of Bedouin women's oral poetry, Moneera al-Ghadeer confirms that this sense of harmony between the desert-tribal and technology-modern exists, even in remote corners of the Arabian Peninsula. These women poets' celebration of the marriage of apparent opposites contrasts with Munif's dystopia in which all that is not desert-tribal threatens. The oral poems, al-Ghadeer writes, "illustrate a feminine desire for the machine ... a dynamic and positive relationship between women and technology" (al-Ghadeer 2009, 147, 148). The car in the desert will return the lover more quickly to the beloved than the camel ever could: "references to the motorcar, aeroplane and binoculars offer a metaphorical inscription of modernity in the desert" (157–58, 190).

PATHOLOGIZING THE GENDER BARZAKH

Loved or feared, technology and rapid social transformations do create tension in the Gulf *barzakh*. Women's education and greater participation in the public sphere threaten men who may use draconian measures to control women's mobility outside the home. Women negotiating the perilous terrain between new opportunities and old constraints have to walk a fine line to hold on to their balance and even, sometimes, their sanity. Some look to professionals for help, while others challenge the system head-on.

Between the spaces of convergence and indeterminacy in the Gulf, a new phenomenon demands attention: a gender *barzakh*. Cross-dressing and queer public performances are attracting official interference. Said to be a violation of Islamic values, homosexuality is outlawed in Gulf Arab states. Consequently, queer activity had gone underground. During the past decade, however, some LGBT men and women have begun to perform their taboo identities publicly, despite fear of retaliation.

In November 2005, Emirati police raided a mass wedding ceremony for twenty-six men and arrested twenty-two of them: "The transvestites were ordered to receive male hormone injections in addition to their prison sentences and within days mobile phone videos that had been recorded by arresting officers were circulating amongst the Dubai national community, thereby tarnishing the family names of those arrested. In most cases, however, these anti-homosexual laws are now flagrantly violated, with openly homosexual men walking around shopping malls, and with certain well known hotel bars and nightclubs serving as de facto 'gay clubs'" (Davidson 2008, 198–99). The first step the government took was medical: the men received male hormone injections. While they were waiting for the drugs to kick in, the police kept the men incarcerated to prevent further chaos. Or, so they said, because the videos the police had produced and then circulated had aggravated an already tense social situation and further dishonored the families.

These male unions are part of an institution known as `*urfi*, or customary marriage. `*Urfi* marriages bypass state regulations, Islamic law, and also social expectations for prohibitively expensive ceremonies. Although these "sexual and gender-'queer' practices and identities are recognized as indigenous" and therefore not in themselves new (Hasso 2011, 11–12, 133), the fact that men are going public with these practices and identities is new. In February 2011, there was another mass arrest, this time in Bahrain, where policing of gays had been less vicious. Two hundred men celebrating a gay wedding in Muharraq were thrown into jail.[6]

Recently, several art projects have focused on queer identities in the Gulf, including Fatima Al Qadiri and Khalid Al Gharaballi's "Mendeel Um Ahmad" (Umm Ahmad's Tissue). This video features three male transvestites: a glamorous Umm Ahmad with her long, auburn wig, a plump school teacher nervously clutching her bag, and a rather sinister third lady at a morning coffee clutch cracking open sunflower seeds under her black wrap. Seated far apart, each with her own little table, they are drinking tea in a soulless, luxurious house somewhere in Kuwait. An Indonesian or Philippine maid in uniform slowly wheels in her trolley of sweetmeats, and the ladies daintily pick out a favorite delicacy without acknowledging her presence. When she leaves, they resume their catty small talk that serves to critique women's superficial, empty lives and their abuse of foreign servants.

BOYAHS

Until recently, it was a matter of: don't ask, don't tell. But the queer community is no longer so ready to comply with mandates for invisibility. With more and more young people coming out in public places, panic has set in, and homosexuality is being pathologized. For example, Qatari Al Aween Center, a "social rehabilitation center" established in May 2009, diagnoses and treats behavioral abnormalities that seem to revolve around LGBT activities and appearance. On July 7, 2011, the online site "Gay Middle East" reproduced the Al Aween Mission: "to protect the normal character against deviation from acceptable social behaviour, treat people with deviant attitudes, develop self-reliance and self-confidence in such people, prevent them from descending to total breakdown and isolation, and work to integrate them in society. It also works to alert the society against deviation and familiarize individuals with their rights and obligations." Lectures hosted at Al Aween include: appearance modification; masculine/feminine behavior; "Figure and style modifications: like long hair for men and men's trousers for girls to clarify the difference [*sic*] aspects between boys and girls;" "Sexual identity disorder/ perturbation[7] . . . or what we call imitating men."[8] In the summer of 2009 Al Aween launched a campaign entitled "My femininity is a gift from my Lord." Lorenz Nigst and Jose Sanchez Garcia comment that although "religion is used to turn an individual choice into a 'deviation' that compromises morality . . . It is worth emphasizing that many of them present themselves as Muslims." Promising to cure young people of these dire diseases, Al Aween designed a program they called "Youth Without Problems" (Nigst and Garcia 2010, 19, 20, 21, 29).

But is it a disease for girls to imitate men? Actually, it can be rather fun.

When Sophia, the Qatari-American heroine of *The Girl Who Fell to Earth*, wonders what she should wear for her birthday party, a relative makes a surprising suggestion.

"You can be a *boyah* for your birthday."

What's a *boyah*? In this coming-of-age memoir, Sophia Al-Maria tells us. Understood to mean tomboy, "The word was so much a part of daily parlance that no one seemed to make the connection that it was just a feminine conjugation of the English word *boy*... Falak cobbled together a costume for me from one of Moody's sons' crisp white *thobes*, a pair of mirrored aviator sunglasses pilfered from Faraj's room, and eyeliner, which she used to draw a mustache. The *gutra* was harder to keep on my head than a *shayla*, and the billowy wide-legged *sirwal* [long underpants for men] made me feel disturbingly exposed." Sophia learns that the *boyah* phenomenon began in universities, where it had evolved into a kind of gang culture: "it became more than drag or inflecting your walk with butch swagger. There is a prismatic range of *boyah* types, from hetero-dabblers to the most earnest bull dyke" (Al-Maria 2012, 134–35). Al-Maria tells the story of her childhood and early adulthood spent between Qatar and the U.S., between two worlds that are at once utterly strange and totally familiar. So, to be dressed like a *boyah* for her special day is another experience of the simultaneously strange and familiar.

Some describe the shock of encountering these girls who look like boys: "The only way I realized they were in actuality girls was because they were in an all Women's beach... Haircut, pitch of voice (*nabra khashina*) and colognes used are deliberately boyish... Sometimes male names are substituted for female names. Sources also mention 'boyish' behavior like bullying" (Nigst and Garcia 2010, 5, 6). With their provocative appearance, *boyahs* (sometimes the plural is *boyat*) attract strong censure, but they seem to enjoy the provocation. In her cutting-edge research on the subject, Noor Al-Qasimi asserts that the *boyah* culture emerges out of "an increasingly visible subculture within the Arab Gulf states. The articulation of *boyat* (plural) in cyberspace, primarily through social networking web sites such as Facebook, Flickr, and MySpace, has created a transnational pan-Gulfian community, with the Internet serving as a mediator for the production of a queer imaginary. While the *boyah* signifies a shared system of cultural representation within the region of the Arab Gulf, national specificity is often articulated within such queer self-stylizations. For example, on Facebook, references to national specificity with *boyat* users is evinced in user names such as 'Boyah Q8 [Kuwait]' and 'Jedda Altomboys'" (Al-Qasimi 2012, 139).

Al-Qasimi analyzes this image made by Fatima Al Qadiri and Khalid Al Gharaballi, the producers of the "Um Ahmad Tissue" video. The cap, she writes, "signifies a common self-stylization of *boyat* as well as Gulf male youth, especially in its combination with the *dishdasha* (male national dress)" (139). The *dishdasha* references Gulf men in general and the cap with its coloring and lettering announces Kuwait.

Not all *boyat* wear the Gulf men's distinctive dress, yet they are immediately recognizable. At the American University in Sharjah, students told me that a *boyah* distinguishes herself by her combat boots or Louis Vuitton wedge shoes or the *thawb/ dishdasha* made of `*abaya* material.[9] They are wearing the national brand against the grain and enjoying the shock they create when they enter public space.

Figure 16. "I Wanna Live" by Fatima Al Qadiri and Khalid Al Gharaballi, *Wa Wa Complex* (2011).

Read Superwoman's blog (March 13, 2010, 10:47 p.m.): "Boyat! Ever heard of this term before? well even if u haven't I'm sure you've seen it: a girl in her abaya walking talking like a man or short hair girl wearing loose jeans and a head band in all dresses wedding. Well this weird phenomenon was here for ages but it was never publicly spoken until recent days, and it's basically homosexuality you know girls liking other girls blah blah blah."[10] So, the *boyah* phenomenon is not new, but even to this hip, vernacular writer it is a problem. It is a problem because for her "it's basically homosexuality." Or, is it?

Nigst and Garcia suggest that the *boyahs* are less about sexual orientation than they are about "transgression of gender norms" in segregated societies with rigid gender rules. This transgression is a problem that can be solved by "pushing girls back into their traditional roles where they again re-embody the social norms and dominant ethical valorizations" (Nigst and Garcia 2010, 9, 23).

Some blame outsiders for encouraging nonconformity with tribal expectations. Others suggest that these rebels are inter-sexed persons who refuse "normal" categorization of male and female and the spaces each should occupy. Considered symptoms of the crisis in societies moving too fast from the morality of their tribal past into an anomic future, *boyahs* create "a new counter-public," an unacceptable gender *barzakh*.

Cross-dressing empowers some young women to leave private places. In occupying public space, they are confusing social codes. Society has to work out how to control these individuals who are acting "as 'different' female beings and as 'different' men at the same time, thus breaking the traditional segregation of the sexes in the use of space" (16, 32). In such a formulation, *boyat* are both men and women, neither men nor women, and also something else.

The state is intervening to regulate appropriate gender identities in a newly configured public sphere. In 2009, the UAE Ministry of Social Affairs "launched an 'awareness initiative' targeting young women within educational institutions and youth detention centers identified as *mustarjilat*, or young women who '[give] up the characteristics of femininity, [try] to imitate boys in clothing and mannerisms, and [are] attracted to females only.' [Some students] are required to sign a *taʿahhud* (agreement) that they will behave [in a sexually appropriate manner]" (Al-Qasimi 2011, 284). With such disciplining of public space, *boyahs* have been turning to the Internet for an alternative space to experience and perform their desired identities. Linking virtual and real space as co-constitutive, Noor Al-Qasimi suggests that "a pan-Gulfian transnational queer imaginary is being produced in the context of new social networking technologies [...] In recent years the proliferation of queer subjectivities in the United Arab Emirates has been detected in greater magnitude, instigating a national moral panic" (Al-Qasimi 2011, 285, 286). So great has the panic become that female police are surveilling women's private, segregated spaces that are thus "resignified, no longer considered private" (289). *Boyahs* are beginning to break down the spatial binaries that have organized post-oil Gulf life. The consequent moral turpitude is blamed on the West, the usual vague scapegoat. Living between socially constructed subjectivities, *boyahs* inhabit a gender *barzakh* that connects and disconnects specific identities, whether female-feminine or male-masculine identities.

WOMEN WRITING IN THE *BARZAKH*

Some women, like the *boyat*, feel defiant and newly empowered; others do not. While social transformations bring freedom and choices, they are also isolating. Material and virtual walls are growing up around native citizens, especially the women, and their houses or family compounds, separating them from the foreign majority but also from their neighbors. Older women brought up in the pre-oil era complain that they can no longer visit each other as they used to in the past. Each visit outside the walls requires dressing appropriately and engaging a driver, since walking in places where they might be seen by outsiders is frowned upon: "What they don't have now is a community life, a sense of living together," writes Bristol-Rhys of women living in Abu Dhabi. A grandmother she interviewed said "the generation born after all the changes, after the money and the building, that is the generation that has lost its way [...] What will they do if this all disappears?" (58, 62) Accustomed to air-conditioning, luxury, summer homes in London or the French Riviera or Sardinia, few are giving this question much thought. The fast-fading past is losing its hold.

Women are writing about their hopes but also their fear of societal disintegration, and anxiety about the tightening of patriarchal strictures. Breaking taboos concerning sex and desire, some escape into writing where women's power can be enjoyed and celebrated. Sheherezade, the heroine and narrator of the *Arabian Nights* whose storytelling saved her life, provides comfort and a sense of discursive power. Qatari Huda al-Nu`aimi is a nuclear physicist who published her first collection of short stories *al-Mikhala* (The Kohl Bottle) in 1997, she celebrates Sheherezade's first night after the 1001st when she controls the fate of Shahrayar with her army of 1001 women from all places and ages.[11] For Raja' `Alim, the *Arabian Nights* inspire girls' imaginations: "No one could stop us from going down into the labyrinth of writing, no one could keep us from being captivated by the subject matter itself" (`Alim 2007, 112, 172, 220, 248). Her magical realist novel *Fatma* (2002) tells the story of a divorced woman's metamorphosis into a snake shepherd and then the snake queen of the tribal kingdom of Najran in Southern Arabia. Bitten by the deadliest of all the snakes, this enchanted snake herder thrives in a poisoned body that produces tattoos as totems liberating her from her husband's violence.

Others critique the patriarchal values of their still-tribal societies in less flamboyant ways. The highly acclaimed Kuwaiti

Laila al-`Uthman (b. 1950) led the way in the 1960s with her short stories that revolve around men's cruelty and women's indifference to their daughters. Recently, she told the tragedy of a young woman whose mother at the point of divorce had rejected her: "Take her! I don't want her!"—the book's title—echoes throughout the 2010 novel. And then we read the daughter's terrible regret while she watches her mother's corpse being washed, embalmed, and shrouded. All those things she wished she had told her mother bubble up painfully. The cycle of violence is relentless, but she senses that had she not let her hurt fester, she might have stopped the recurrence of the violence.

Al-Nu`aimi writes of the loneliness of women who become anonymous trophies on their wedding day.[12] The death of an embryo after its father had beaten its mother signals a negative form of salvation: the baby has been saved the fate of growing up to be an abusive father or an abused mother. Worse still, this baby might have grown up to be like the man who ripped out his mother's heart, licked it clean, and gave it to his beloved Anna Karenina. Saudi Khayriyya al-Saqqaf (b. 1951) writes about a woman whose family robs her of all she owns and then arranges for her to be thrown into prison on trumped-up charges (al-Saqqaf 1998, 69–72).

These women's writings reflect the "shift from a tribal society to a modern state (that) has undermined the traditional individual function of protector as a member of a tribe, not only vis-à-vis other male members but, more importantly, vis-à-vis women" (Arebi 1994, 272). The fact that women make up 70 percent of Gulf university student bodies means that they are poised to become the majority of white-collar workers in a future when Emiratization, Qatarization, Bahrainization, and Kuwaitization policies have been implemented—at least, that is the hope. These women have been educated to be independent, to know their rights and to know when they are being withheld; they are also caught between two worlds that they are learning to negotiate and bridge.

THE TERRIBLE COLD

Tropes of misogyny are not new in Arab women's writings, but what is different in some Gulf Arab women's stories and poems is the recurrence of mortal cold. How odd that bitter cold has become a theme in such a terribly hot region. Unlike their sisters in the desert who composed odes to the car and the aeroplane that they welcome into their old world, these urban women writers struggle in the new world that technology has produced. Its major effect is coldness.

Al-Saqqaf writes about an inhuman, morgue-like atmosphere. She fears this icy cold that is freezing the heat of the desert. In one of her stories, a pilgrim is caught in a freezing flash flood. He is returning to Jeddah from Mecca where he has just performed the `umra, a rite next only to the *Hajj* in terms of Islamic duty and spiritual sanctity. He is stranded on the roadside and there is no Good Samaritan willing to come to his aid. No one in this crisis will help him without first exacting an exorbitant price (al-Saqqaf 1989, 440–44). In another short story, a two-page vignette, al-Saqqaf evokes the sterility of an air-conditioned apartment. It is only when the unit breaks down, the whirring stops, and the heat returns, that she can breathe again.

In 1989, Saudi Sharifa Shamlan (b. 1946) published her tragic story about a lost servant. The family rummages around the house in annoyance. How dare she put them to this much trouble! To their surprise and dismay they finally find her in the freezer, "frozen into a mannequin of ice. Who closed the freezer door on Zainab? But that is another matter" (Shamlan 1998, 41). Women servants do not belong in the warmth of the family home. We can hear echoes from other women writers. Is this not reminiscent of the sympathy for the migrant laborers pervading Al Subaiey's poem about the broken souls of the invisible army that has built the glittering new Gulf cities? The cruelty servants endure is etched in ice. "Refrigerator" by Kuwaiti Saadia Mufarreh (b. 1965) is another articulation of the ice that has seized some women's souls. In this poem Mufarreh has internalized the trope of cold:

> I opened it
> Its contents were tidy
> Bottles of preserved milk
> Cartons of yogurt
> Bags of frozen meat
> Yellow apples
> Medicine, bread
> And … and … etc.
> In the refrigerator of my soul
> The contents scatter
> And expire
> And remain closed.
>
> Paine, Lodge, and Touati 2011, 110

This terrible cold has seeped from the outside to the inside of a woman who has managed social expectations. She looks organized: she has carefully stashed away food and drink and medicine. But this tidiness, this concern for the welfare of others is contained in the coffin case of her soul. And inside there, in the locked refrigerator of her soul we see the truth: the veil of appearances is rent asunder to reveal her spiritual death by freezing. The exactions of modernity have brought a merciless cold, that then becomes the metonym for modernity.

One of Huda al-Nu`aimi's protagonists declares that women spend their life in "an old refrigerator" (al-Nu`aimi 2001, 64). In this version, women are outside modernity, in an old-fashioned refrigerator whence they watch the world pass them by. Qatari Amina al-Imadi's short story "The Cold Sun" captures the oxymoron in the title. The inversion of the natural world haunts these women's writings. The burning sun of the desert is turned into a freezing agent. Tribal norms and values disappear in the cold of the sun in a family that refuses to care for its grandparents, preferring to send them to spend their last days in an old people's institution (Ramsay 2003, 372).

Although less cruel in its depiction of the generational disconnect between elders born in tents and their children comfortable only in A/C, Emirati Maryam Al Saedi's "The Old Woman" paints a sad picture of the last years in the life of a Bedouin woman. Her sons and daughters have left the desert to take up lucrative professions. They live in the comfort of the city. Seeing their mother in the tent in which they were born, they cannot imagine that she might wish to stay there. One after another they invite her to stay in their air-conditioned homes: "In the older son's house she found the room cold, the bedding cold, and the house cold [. . .] When it became very cold she wanted to move to another son's house, then to another's and yet another's. Then to one daughter's and to another daughter's and to another's. She moved between them all and found all their houses too cold" (Johnson-Davies 2009, 61). With little choice in the matter, she finally remains in one of these houses, unwilling to continue the round of visits to her children. But in this last urban dwelling, she refuses to leave her room or to eat anything but bread and yogurt. Slowly but surely she starves to death. At the mourning reception, everyone admires her sons and daughters who did, after all, what they could for the crazy old woman.

In her poem "Body's Winter," Emirati Khulood Al Mu'alla, in four short lines, juxtaposes again the sun and the cold:

> The sun pierces every detail
> Nothing casts a shadow
> Everything is burning
> And this body is still cold
>
> Paine, Lodge, and Touati 2011, 304

It is not only the A/C that chills those used to the burning heat of the desert sun. In this new world it is the sun itself that freezes women's bodies and souls.

Saudi Nimah Ismail Nawwab's poem about forced divorce likens the life of these persecuted lovers to imprisonment in a cold cell, to burial in the cold of a living tomb. Her 2007 poem written for Fatimah, the victim of forced divorce, evokes the crisis in images of cold and death:

> The cold cell closes in
> The cold of a living tomb
> every breath a test
> every breath a labor
> every breath a prayer...

The chilly prison
more merciful
    than the icy
      hard

        hearts
        of family.
      seeking to sever her bonds of love
            in *Arab News*

"Awakening" by Bahraini Fawzia Al Sindi is another poem to describe the freezing heat:

My limbs are exhausted from the cold sun
panting after the dead stone.
O, frigid stone, my limbs
pierce me, they are enflamed
by a bewildering chill like the strong arms
of a future nation...
Awaken, for a sweet numbness gathers in my limbs and
    sharpens me
like a spear plunging in the heart's folds, exploding arteries
of words. Awaken, my voice is not capable of whispering.
It weeps blood,
the perfume of the seventies,
its comrades haunted by stabs
of doubt. I read only the soil
of the past, my blood is taken from me

           Paine, Lodge, and Touati 2011, 16–17

Cold sun, frigid stone, and a bewildering chill that enflames; such is the currency of Al Sindi's awakening. She knows she must speak but she is numb, incapable even of whispering. The cold sun tortures her. The cold sun flings the poet into the strong arms of a frightening future nation. The answer is to

Figure 17. Hala Al Khalifa's *Anxiety of Place (Qalaq al-makan)*.

become numb and to return to the sweetness of the revolutionary past, even when knowing that one must awaken to reality. Piercing and stabbing, reality tries to destroy her and she, the poet, has lost her one weapon, her voice. She cannot even whisper to warn the world of the terrors in store for it. Nostalgia makes her voice bleed.

These icy worlds figure in literature, but also in art. In 2009, Bahraini artist Hala Al Khalifa (b. 1975) opened her "Fragments of Memory" solo show in Doha that showcased a series of semi-abstract canvases entitled *Qalaq al-makan*, or Anxiety of Place. Each painting suggested a woman, her head encased in an ice helmet with streaks of red dripping down through icy vapors billowing around the body in its suit of armor. Each painting might have been an illustration of one for these stories.

CONCLUDING WITH THE EGYPTIAN DESERT

While many Gulf women have written poems about tribalism and the difficulty of balancing its norms and values with those of the modern world, it is an Egyptian woman who has narrated such experiences in a novel. Miral al-Tahawy (b. 1968) explores the confusing *barzakh* of the tribal modern that connects and disconnects Egyptian tribes with their Arabian relatives. In an interview with 'Azmi 'Abdallah of Egypt's *Al-Ahram* newspaper, al-Tahawy talked about her Bedouin family and the "question of identity and the notion of tribal belonging, of ethnic purity and the taboos of early youth."[13] Trying to negotiate a future that will hold on to the values of both while refusing to be bound by them, her protagonists struggle with multiple contradictions.

Her fiction links the Egyptian Bedouin to their kin scattered throughout the Arabian Peninsula. *The Tent* (1996) narrates the semi-autobiographical story of Fatima who grows up in an oasis of the Egyptian Eastern Desert. The women and their "abundant generosity" are exotic with their tattoos, silver-capped teeth, gold belts, fat silver bracelets, and heavy perfumes. They spin wool and weave it into carpets; they dance, "laughed and smeared their heels with ash, and rubbed oil onto the palms of their hands." These women consult "soothsayers and sand readers and old women who burned incense and recited spells" (al-Tahawy 2000, 55, 80). Into this world of magic steps the English anthropologist Anne who saves Fatima's life by having her leg amputated after the horned viper bit her (reminiscent of 'Alim's Fatima who was also bitten by such a snake). She takes Fatima to her home where she teaches her English, French, and the three Rs, and turns her into a native informant. Frozen into a folkloric replica for the amusement of visitors, Fatima becomes a human heritage project. One day, however, she rebels: "I am not a frog in a crystal jar for you to gaze upon... Don't applaud Fatim the cripple. I'm not going to sing. I'm not going to perform Bedouin folk songs" (107). Lost between the tribal and the modern, she does not want to be "split in two, one half jabbering away in foreign languages and the other singing traditional Bedouin folk songs" (117).

A later novel, al-Tahawy's 2008 *Gazelle Tracks* tells the story of a tribe amputated from its kinship network that used to connect the deserts of Egypt, Jordan, Syria, and the Arabian Peninsula. The days of glory have passed for the Egyptians, and the shaikh snatches at their tattered fringes. Nostalgia hovers over the memories of their estates along the Nile and the "royal decree confirming the tribe's guardianship of the Nile caravans" (al-Tahawy 2008, 21). When Nasser expropriated all landowners, the shaikh wrote to King Faisal Bin Abdulaziz Al Saud begging him to authorize the return of his tribe to their ancestral lands in the Najd. Was he not married to the daughter of al-Najdiyya, the woman from Kafr al-Zayyat, whose name indicated her origin in the heartland of Saudi Arabia? They had, after all, demonstrated their loyalty to the Saudis through good and bad times. The king did not respond to the request.

The once-splendid but now empty stables hold on to the memories. Visiting Saudi and Kuwaiti princes are surprised "that there were still Arab tribes in this part of the world that maintained the genealogies and lines of their horses" (25). Like their Gulf Arab kin, they love horses, and even though they no longer have horses they dream "of reviving the Bedouin heritage by building a racetrack where the fillies could run against one another with the salukis bounding behind them" (18). But their dream is just a dream. Unlike their kin in the Gulf, these Egyptian Bedouins do not have the wherewithal to realize such a dream in a mechanized racetrack. The tribal network no longer matters in a world where tribal shaikhs have become rulers of new nation-states. Those who continue to believe in the networks are deluded. If the heritage cannot be revived materially, it might be saved symbolically, and so the heroine's father imagines "starting a newspaper in the tribe's name whose slogan would be: 'Bedouinism: the origin of civilization'" (26). But his tribal values and practices are disappearing. The young do not even know how to hold themselves in a manner appropriate for members of an elite tribe. His daughter is so acculturated that she has been instructed to learn "how to sit like a Bedouin woman (because) she was a daughter of the Arabs, a true desert thoroughbred" (6, 7). Social outcasts living on the margins of modern society, Egyptian Bedouin do not share the Gulf Arabs' privilege. They cannot go back to the dream of braiding twin belongings of tribe and nation into modernity.

Conclusion

We talk of many things we don't understand.
Modernity in the desert! The latest
joke in a world full of jokes.
But this is the desert,
where dust hovers in the air like butterflies
in a graveyard.
Where sand blankets everything—
acacia and palms, the tents
of Bedouins, even camels,
the ships of the dunes.

So little can grow in the desert.

Our palaces scream cutting-edge.
Our A/C's hiss like snakes.
Cell phones! Cyber cafés!

But remember, the desert is a fox
dressed like a woman.

Soad Al Kuwari (Paine, Lodge, and Touati 2011)

For Qatari Soad Al Kuwari, modernity in the desert, the tribal modern, is a joke in a world full of jokes. Screaming, hissing, the cold, plastic emblems of modernity have appeared in the sepulchral desert. They are foxes dressed like women.

Throughout this book, I have used the words of poets and writers to anchor my analysis of the tribal modern. Creative writers and artists are always ahead of trends, able to see beyond the confusion reigning during times of change. It was the poets, short story writers, and graffiti artists who were making sense of the 2011 Arab Spring when political scientists and sociologists were struggling to make the unprecedented fit into their pre-fixed molds. In the same way, Gulf Arab poets and fiction writers have captured a particular dynamic of life in the *barzakh* that has escaped social scientists' paradigms.

In the swirl of radical social transformation, Gulf Arabs are projecting a distinctive national and cultural brand identity that is rooted, ancient, and tribal but also transnational, modern, and cosmopolitan. Before oil their countries were unlivable, but today they have the wealth and power to assure luxurious lifestyles, continued independence, and growing international presence.

In some cases, oil and natural gas are no longer the only, necessary engines of change and prosperity. In late November 2012, *Khaleej Times* published an article about Dubai's exceptional growth that was due to diversification in "trade, tourism, logistics, FDI [foreign direct investment], exports and re-exports, which traditionally formed the bedrock of Dubai's evolution into a global hub. The hotel and restaurant industry witnessed more than 16 percent growth, while manufacturing expanded 10.4 percent." In the first half of 2012, five million tourists visited and

Figure 18. Cultural Essence of Qatar Café (photo by Samia
Serageldin).

stayed in Dubai ... Passenger traffic through Dubai International
Airport increased 13.7 percent. By 2015, the airport is projected to
handle 75 million passengers."

Economic growth has encouraged exporting the brand.
Recently, some Gulf states have invested in twenty-first-century
Britain, their erstwhile protector/colonizer. Where better to
market the national brand than in the heart of the former empire?
In 2010, Qatar Holding—part of the emirate's sovereign wealth
fund that was set up in 2005 to diversify its investments away
from oil and gas—bought the iconic department store Harrods
for almost three billion pounds Sterling. In the spring of 2012,
Harrods opened the Cultural Essence of Qatar hall with a café

Figure 19. Qatar Gallery at Harrods with saleswomen (photo by
Samia Serageldin).

displaying the elements of that essence: a wall full of identical
coffeepots.

When the Moroccan and Lebanese saleswomen were asked
what distinguished this cultural essence, they were stumped,
waving their hands in the direction of books about horses and
falcons and dhows.

Two years later, Qatar Holding announced a further development. They are planning to build a Harrods hotel chain in
key cities such as London, Kuala Lumpur, New York, and Paris,
as well as in Sardinia, "And if that last one has you scratching
your head, it's because Sardinia's Costa Smeralda in fact belongs
to the company."[1]

Qatar's former Emir Hamad Al Thani was described as "fast becoming a kingmaker in British property development, snapping up a series of trophy sites in the past five years including Chelsea Barracks, the luxury apartment complex at One Hyde Park, the US embassy in Grosvenor Square and the Olympic Village."[2] All of these properties are remarkable, but most extraordinary is the acquisition of the US embassy building. What does it mean for one country to own another country's embassy in another country?

In 2013, the state announced a year to "celebrate the cultures of Qatar and the United Kingdom through the exchange of knowledge, arts, sports, film, and other engaging mediums. The two nations share innovative ideas and practices, encouraging talent and creativity across both societies and this will be the platform leading to new long-term partnerships between institutions and generating more engagement between the people of Qatar and the UK." It is hoped that the focus on culture, sports, and education will "promote the mutual understanding, recognition and appreciation of the Qatari and British cultures, traditions and people." Above all, the explicit goal is to "showcase and promote modern Qatar, and promote Arab language and culture more broadly in [the] UK (and to) celebrate Qatar as hosts of the FIFA World Cup 2022."[3] With a tip of the hat to the need for the Qataris to appreciate British culture—which they already do—the agenda was set. It is time for the British to acknowledge the importance of Qatari culture. They also want to attract investors—and they are.[4] The bulk of the investment, however, is by Qatar in the United Kingdom.

Qatari investment in Europe and in Britain has been considerable. In 2012 alone, Qatar spent $4.3 billion on European property.[5] Symbolically poignant in this politically significant real-estate grab is their purchase of the Raffles Hotel in Singapore, the emblem par excellence of the British imperial past. What better way to market the tribal modern brand than to buy, shape, and transform the symbol of colonial British luxury and power in Southeast Asia into yet another Qatari exhibit.

With this real estate in hand, the Qatari state is now acquiring global economic power. On October 4, 2012, the *Gulf Times* announced that the Qatar Chamber of Commerce had launched a global initiative aimed at "bringing the world together to shape a new trade agreement for the 21st century." The next day, the paper reported that Qatar Holding wanted to add a majority commodity stake in Morgan Stanley to its investments in European firms, which include Credit Suisse Group and Xstrata, a Switzerland-based mining company.

Economic power has spawned political power in the wake of the Arab uprisings of 2010–2012, with Qatar taking the lead. After playing a decisive role in the revolutions in Libya and Yemen, the Emir Shaikh Hamad bin Khalifa Al Thani announced, at the September 2012 U.N. Assembly, a Qatari initiative to intervene in the Syrian conflict. Where the U.N. had failed, he planned to succeed. In early November, he followed up on that promise when he convened a five-day meeting of Syrian opposition factions. This marked the first attempt to bring opposition groups based abroad together with rebels fighting in Syria. The outcome of that meeting was the formation of the National Coalition for Syrian Revolutionary and Opposition Forces, which France almost immediately recognized as the Syrian people's sole legitimate representative. A few days later, Qatar invited the newly formed coalition to name an ambassador. It was the first state to do so, and on February 14, 2013, it was the first of the so-called Friends of Syria Coalition, which includes Britain and France, to hand over the Syrian embassy building to the opposition.

During the past eighteen months, Qatar has invested heavily in the new Arab states. Qatar Petroleum has pumped $2 billion into Tunisia where it is building oil refineries. The former Emir "promised Egypt financial aid totaling $5 billion, on top of plans to invest another $18 billion in the country over the next five years." Then, on Wednesday [April 10, 2013], it sent yet another lifeline, pledging to boost the struggling economy by buying up $3 billion in government bonds. It also offered to send gas to stave off expected summer blackouts, which will give Morsi some much-needed political relief. The announcement of the sudden cash influx came as a shock to many Egyptians. "Qatar has effectively annexed Egypt as of this morning," Bassem Sabry, a writer and blogger, tweeted as news of the loan broke."[6] An Egyptian friend suggested wryly that the next thing to go to the Qataris would be the great pyramids.

It is not only in new areas of conflict that the former Emir intervened; he also turned his attention and treasury to the seemingly unresolvable Israel–Palestine hostilities. He committed $400 million to rebuild infrastructure in Gaza. On October 23, 2012, he "became the first head of state to visit the Gaza Strip since Hamas wrested control of it in 2007, the latest step in an ambitious campaign by the tiny Gulf nation to leverage its outsize pocketbook in support of Islamists across the region."[7]

Regional power has inspired global ambitions. On February 12, 2013, *The Peninsula* reported that the Prime Minister had "called for an overhaul of the United Nations and its Security Council, as also of the Arab League, saying it was time these key organizations were reformed to keep pace with the changing times and social and political realities." Qatar has become a regional powerhouse wedding economic and political power to cultural power.

Culture, previously blamed for the failure to modernize, is now the privileged site for forging modernity. These heirs to spiritual (birth of Islam in the Peninsula) and material (oil and natural gas) blessings beyond the dreams of Sheherezade are now turning to culture—museums, education cities, artists' colonies, film industries, and jazz festivals—to ground their feverish modernization projects in an authenticity not available to those who live on this land but will never be of it. A tribal modern subjectivity is emerging out of a deeply local sense of historical place and a wide-ranging vision of a role in the world. The culturally inflected brand is becoming more visible because it is widely advertised.[8] Newly established national and cultural separateness was recognized in 1998 when Abu Dhabi and Sharjah—with its biennial motto of Tradition and Modernity—were named Capitals of Arab Culture. Doha followed suit in 2010. Cultural uniqueness is being fabricated out of whole cloth to distinguish new countries from each other but also from their past. The challenge is to mesh individual memories of belonging to an unbounded territory with official histories of borders and flags.

First, regional uniqueness. Next, national distinctiveness. Then, transnational fame. For Qatar, the national museum—with its desert-rose-cum-spaceship motif—the Museum of Islamic Art, Suq Waqif, and Al-Jazeera satellite television shape the national brand. For the UAE, the future national museum in Abu Dhabi with its falcon-based design, the sail-cum-kandura-shaped, seven-star Burj al-'Arab hotel and the world's tallest building, the Burj Khalifa in Dubai, braid the modern and the tribal together into national distinctiveness.[9]

Heritage projects are the cornerstone of the Gulf states' authentification of modernizing processes. These projects forget the bad and the ugly from a desperately poor past that relied on the punishing labor of pastoral nomads, desert agriculturalists, and pearl divers. They recuperate the good and the beautiful from a rapidly disappearing pre-oil world. In the process, heritage revival becomes "not a negation of globalization but rather an affirmation of it" (Khalaf 2002, 14). Balancing allegiances to tribe and nation-state, today's Gulf Arabs are tribal nationalists crafting a modern identity.

The affirmation of tribal identities has gone global, and indigenous people, from South Asia to the Americas, are demanding recognition and often also compensation for past exploitation. The greater the economic incentive, the more urgent does it become for indigenous inhabitants to assert genetic rights in order to limit others' access to the wealth they consider theirs. Wealth and power differentiate Gulf Arab tribes from indigenous groups elsewhere that have recently come together to claim ancestral rights, yet they share concerns. In India, for example, debates revolve around "why and how members of 'tribes', political leaders as well as government officers construct 'tribal' authenticity in a politicized arena, and how this relates to the social and cultural realities 'on the ground.'" (Schleiter and de Maaker 2010, 16). Although the *adivasi* Indian tribes are differently situated, they too are embracing the possibilities of the *barzakh* in which the tribal and the modern mix and separate. Gregory Allen uses the term "tribal chic" to describe the ways in which individual dress and style cross the border that connects and disconnects "tradition and modernity—or hypermodernity, late modernity, or postmodernity, the 'West' and the indigenous" (Allen 2012, 631). This style, he writes, "may seem to us to juxtapose incongruities, but does it? I think this sense of a border crossing says more about our perceptions than it does about *adivasis*. The style crosses borders because it juxtaposes what is familiar *to me* with what is unfamiliar" (651, my emphasis).

This is precisely my point: from the perspective of the outsider, the tribal and the modern seem incongruous together. From this perspective, their combination appears to be a loss of tradition and a failure to modernize. In this book, I have attempted to reverse that gaze in order to see how the idea of the tribe, rather than any false notion of tribes' biological persistence into the present, has enabled a form of hypermodernity.

The tribal modern is the *barzakh* that connects and disconnects a specific, separate, superior, uncontaminated identity from the cosmopolitan mandates of the twenty-first century. The tribal is the new aristocratic in the flattening anonymity of twenty-first-century transnational movement and cosmopolitanism.

I give the closing words to Dubai poet Khalid Albudoor, whose longing for the lost nomadic past vividly prefigures the tribal modern:

> We wait for no one
> You might say
> No more Bedouins
> They disappeared
> All of them
> Before we knew them
> Or wrote their names

On the skins of our tent
Before we learned love from them
And I would say
Look carefully
Behind our dune
I can see their souls approach us
Rising from the mirage of distance
Or
Appearing to us from
The future.

> Paine, Lodge, and Touati 2011, 351

These lost Bedouins, these specters from the past, are in fact the future of a brave new world, the brave new tribal modern world of tomorrow's Arab Gulf.

ACKNOWLEDGMENTS

Many people have helped me think through the challenges of this book. Some have enabled research in the region, some have invited me to give talks on the tribal modern, and some have read sections of the manuscript as it was taking form. I have dedicated this book to Muhammad 'Ali 'Abdullah and DD Dewar, two artists who gave me extraordinary help and appreciation for Qatari culture during my six months in Doha as scholar-in-residence at the Museum of Islamic Art.

In the Gulf, Shaikh Hasan Al Thani, Amel Saadi Cherif, Yazan Kopty, Patty Paine, and Mohanalakshmi Rajakumar; Jocelyn S. Mitchell, Amira Sonbol, and the VCUQ students in the Muslim Networks class; Pernille Arenfeldt, Noor Al-Qasimi, May Al Khalifa, Qassim Haddad, Fawzia Al Sindi, Siham Al Foraih, and Nimah Ismail Nawwab. I am especially grateful to Sulayman Khalaf for his jocular embrace of the term "tribal modern" and entertaining engagement with the concept. I am deeply indebted to his work.

At Dartmouth College, Marlene Heck, Kevin Reinhart, Zeynep Turkyilmaz, and Maral Yessayan have engaged me in lively conversations.

At Duke University, Ron Batson, Claudia Koonz, Jamal Laith Dillman-Hasso, Walter Mignolo, Charlie Piot, Kristine Stiles, and Diala Alqadi.

Thanks also to Elliott Colla, Judith Tucker, Jale Parla, Murat Belge, Michael Beard, Recep Senturk, Tony Greenwood, Jonathan Cross, and Samia Serageldin.

My sincerest thanks to Shaykha Mayassa Al Thani, enthusiastic student, inspired follower of Leo the African, and generous sponsor over several years. Her love of art has turned Qatar into a vibrant cultural center.

But more than anyone, Bruce Lawrence has been my indispensable companion and critic. He has read every word, more than once, and as always, and again and again, he has encouraged me in my less secure moments.

NOTES

INTRODUCTION

1. Opened two years later on January 4, 2010, the Burj Khalifa "Vertical Odyssey" publicity video hails "an extraordinary testimony of how great icons and landmarks are created…a monument to passion, courage, ambition and leadership [in a] vertical city that prides itself on making the impossible possible" (http://www.burjkhalifa.ae, accessed June 12, 2012). On May 4, 2013, *Gulf Today* reported that Dubai is "home to the tallest residential skyscraper cluster in the world… and the tallest hotel in the world (JW Marriott Marquis)."

2. The men's white robe is called *thawb* in Qatar, *dishdasha* in Kuwait, and *kandura* in the Emirates; the women's black cloak is called `*abaya* in each country.

3. I am aware of the problems surrounding the use of the word "tribe," especially by Africanists. However, I use the word because, for Gulf Arabs, the Arabic term *qabila* (meaning tribe) denotes pride in lineage. In response to a question on primary identity included in a survey on tribes and their status that students of mine conducted, one male responded that his identity was first and foremost "*qabaliya*," that is, tribal, an adjective derived from *qabila*. One of my Virginia

Commonwealth University Qatar (VCUQ) students wrote in her paper on tribal research: "The Qatari community is structured by tribes (she used the plural word *qaba'il*) and these tribes are divided into different major categories.

4. In the two-volume catalogue for the exhibition, William Rubin calls primitivism an "aspect of the history of modern art, not of tribal art." Yet, he retains the word tribal in the subtitle of the exhibition. The equivalence of tribal and primitive became normative. See http://www.nytimes.com/1984/10/28/arts/gallery-view-discovering-the-heart-of-modernism.html?pagewanted=all, accessed January 12, 2013.

5. http://www.huffingtonpost.com/g-roger-denson/internationally-renowned_b_2805629.html, accessed March 5, 2013 (with thanks to Kristine Stiles for bringing this essay to my attention). Marianna Torgovnick links the MoMA exhibition to Tarzan and body piercing (1990).

6. In the final chapter, he follows the 1976 Mashpee Wampanoag Tribal Council trial that was suing in federal court for possession of some land in Cape Cod. The confusion between the tribal and the primitive in the analysis of the "'Primitivism' in 20th Century Art" exhibition has here been replaced with cultural specificity (277–346).

CHAPTER 1

1. Conversation with Shaikha May Al Khalifa, Muharraq, November 30, 2008. In the Gilgamesh epic, Utnapishtim lives in Dilmun after the gods made him and his wife gods for having survived the Flood. Gilgamesh journeys to Dilmun in the hopes that Utnapishtim will grant him immortality, but he fails two tests that would have qualified him. He leaves the land of the immortals and accepts the fact that he will only live on through the material structures he has commissioned.

2. "Artifacts found in Tel Abrak, between Sharjah and Ajman, suggest that there was established trade with the Indus Valley and Ur by 2000 BCE" (Bristol-Rhys 2011, 119; see also Al Ghabban et al. 2010, 14; D. T. Potts 2010, 180–183).

3. http://www.crystalinks.com/dilmun.html, accessed November 13, 2010.

4. Harran is probably Dhahran, the Saudi Arabian port city on the Gulf, location of Aramco, Saudi Arabian Oil Company. It was founded in 1933 when the Saudi government granted Socal, Standard Oil of California, a concession to drill.

5. Fadia Basrawi's father, an early Aramco employee, told her about life on the Arab compound of Aramco in the 1940s: "Our houses in 1944 were little better than stables for camels, very primitive and very insulting. There was a hole in the ground for a toilet and one single light bulb hung from the ceiling. Some rooms didn't have a proper roof, just palm fronds woven together. In summer we boiled from the heat and when the *shamals* came we covered our bodies and faces with wet cloths so we could breathe. Of course in the winter we froze while the Americans were bedded and fed on Aramco's account in large furnished, climate-controlled bungalows" (Basrawi 2009, 92).

6. Arjun Appadurai observes that the transformation in modernity of space into local places is "inherently colonizing, in the sense that it involves the assertion of socially (often ritually) organized power over places and settings that are viewed as potentially chaotic or rebellious" (Appadurai 1996, 181, 183).

7. Warning heeded, the Saudi government made profit-sharing deals with the Americans and in 1980 took full control of Aramco.

8. Writing about Asian migrants to Canada, Sunera Thobani evokes the same scenario: "Despite the recruitment of many such undesired migrants as cheap labour by employers, the prevailing ideology ... fantasized nefarious motives and imagined Asians as plotting to swamp and invade their society" (Thobani 2007, 87).

9. Thobani again draws attention to a similar phenomenon: "when their labour was recognized as necessary for economic development, these migrants were reviled and cast in the figure of the unassimilable and degenerate stranger ... their categorization as non-preferred races constituted them as unworthy of citizenship and minimized the value of their labour" (Thobani 2007, 90).

10. In a student's class project "Origin," the daughter of a Lebanese man given Qatari citizenship because of his special service to the Emir talked to the film's director about her identity. One of the very few foreigners to enjoy the benefits of Qatari citizenship and brought up in the country, she still feels an outsider. In the film, she watches her friends discuss among themselves how foreign she looks despite her Qatari language and affect. She smiles throughout but later confides that she often feels rejected. Almost as an afterthought, she tells Hind that she is more loyal to Qatar than many Qataris. Wistfully, she sighs, "It's nice to feel you belong somewhere." It is not clear whether she means she does or does not belong.

11. *Khaleej Times*, December 14, 2009 (quoted in Fromherz 2012, 9).

12. Shaikha, an old woman from the Qatari royal family, told Hind "before oil, no foreigners came. You never saw strangers" ("Origin").

CHAPTER 2

1. "Origin" (student class project, dir. 2005).

2. Each of Abu Dhabi's rulers between 1761 and 1855 was assassinated, but only three of the seven rulers between 1855 and 2004 were killed. Violence was most intense in the early nineteenth century.

3. Rugh writes that the British may have "made these chiefs more powerful than they could have become on their own" (Rugh 2007, 11).

4. For a discussion of borders in the Arab Gulf, see Schofield 1997, 127–165.

5. "The fact that modern state borders have divided tribes and confined branches of them within state boundaries has contributed to the deterioration of the tribal system as it functioned before modernity" (Sonbol 2012, 333). I would argue that the tribal system has not deteriorated as a result; it has changed.

6. For a vivid account of eighteen months spent in the Empty Quarter with the Al `Azab clan of the Al Murrah, see Cole 1975.

7. In 1922, the British drew a line across the neck of the Qatar peninsula so that their protectorate would be safe from the Saudis. Several

border agreements were subsequently signed (O'Sullivan 2008, 213, 220; see also Schofield 1997, 156).

8. Some claim that Emirati men marry foreigners because of the exorbitant costs of Emirati–Emirati marriages (Bristol-Rhys 2011, 87–88). However, Gulf Arab men and women have long married non-nationals and continue to do so (Ahmad 2012, 17).

9. "To the extent that nation-building was a project that aimed at keeping 'Kuwait to the Kuwaitis,' women were the most committed participants in it" (Longva 1997, 217).

10. Written in Arabic and English, the survey had three sections that asked gender, name, information about the extent of the tribe in time and space, and "the role of the tribe today and whether there is a difference between the tribe and the family. The last section consists of questions that measure the influence of tribal habits and thoughts in social relations, marriage and dress (`abaya* and *thawb*)." The survey was distributed online though Facebook and Twitter and was taken down after five days. Sixty-seven responses were received but only thirty were complete.

11. In *Gazelle Tracks*, an Egyptian novel by the Bedouin Miral al-Tahawy, the tribal shaikh assures his daughter that even "if the King of Egypt himself came to ask for your hand in marriage, I'd chase him away like a dog. Fatim comes from a long line of noble folk" (al-Tahawy 2000, 32–33).

12. "Interpreting *kafa'a* for the bride has been explained in many ways over the course of Islamic history: similarity in religion, social background, wealth, education, even nationality, have all been used as possible bases for *kafa'a*. For the construction of tribal 'nobility,' Hashim and Quraysh became central to the legitimacy of empires" (Sonbol 2012, 320).

13. *Encyclopaedia of Islam*, second edition. http://referenceworks.brill online.com/entries/encyclopaedia-of-islam-2/kafaa-SIM_3772?s .num=13, accessed May 26, 2012. (Content available with subscription or purchase.) `Abd al-Rahman al-Jazairi writes that only Maliki law is not concerned with tribal status. Hanafi, Shafii, and Hanbali schools

call for hypergamy for women and disallow marriage between `*arab* and `*ajam* (or, Persian). Men are generally free to marry whomever they want (al-Jazairi 1969, 54–61). Thanks to Kevin Reinhart for drawing my attention to tribal equivalence in Islamic jurisprudence.

14. The Ideation Center of the management consultancy firm Booz & Company reported GCC divorce statistics: "in Saudi Arabia reached 20% in 2008, 24% in Bahrain in 2007, 25.62% in the UAE in 2008, 34.76% in Qatar in 2009 and 37.13% in Kuwait in 2007." See http://www .arabianbusiness.com/education-pushing-up-gulf-divorce-rates -361201.html, accessed November 11, 2010.

15. "The Fate of Our Protected Saudi Women," in *Middle East Times*, April 2007. http://www.missionandjustice.org/the-fate-of-our -protected-saudi-women-asia-womens-rights/, accessed July 10, 2013.

16. Qatar's codification of family law in 2006 makes "tests for inherited conditions mandatory" (Welchman 2012, 381).

17. The concern to find a pure tribal ancestry is international, and new sites provide easy ways to trace one's DNA; for example, "DNA Tribes: Genetic Ancestry Analysis" allows individuals to compare their "DNA to a world database of over 1000 world ethnic groups" (see http://www.dnatribes.com/index.html, accessed March 9, 2012). For an analysis of the problems inherent in the search for roots through DNA testing, see Alex van Stipriaan, "Testing Roots: A Heritage Project of Body and Soul," in Halbertsma, van Stipriaan, and van Ulzen 2011, 165–187.

CHAPTER 3

1. For example, in 1960, Doha's population was 15,000, in 1980 it was 190,000, and in the 2012 census it had escalated to 1,795,828. (http://www .qsa.gov.qa/eng/PopulationStructure.htm, accessed January 10, 2012).

2. *Elaph*, a Saudi news portal, wrote about the Emir of Qatar's attempts to give depth to his lineage in an eight-million-dollar, thirty-two-episode Ramadan soap opera. Abdullah al-Shammari dismissed the Al Thani claim to Bani Tamim tribal leadership because, unlike

other tribes, it did not have a leader. "The logic goes that since the Bani Tamim, who come from Najd in central Saudi Arabia and whose descendants include the Al Thanis of Qatar, do not have a leader, the mantle is up for grabs" (Al-Qassemi 2012).

3. A similar process informed the foundation of the Al Muhannadi tribe. In the late nineteenth century, during a time of intertribal strife, several tribes banded together to ward off an enemy. Before going to war, they swore allegiance to each other, their hands on a *muhannad* (Arabic for Indian) sword. Since that time they have been known as the Al Muhannadi (conversation with Hissa Al Muhannadi, Doha, November 2, 2010). Amira Sonbol writes that "Arab tribes trace their lineages toward what gives them greater power or prestige" (Sonbol 2012, 319).

4. In Miral al-Tahawy's Egyptian Bedouin novel *Gazelle Tracks*, the last shaikh of an elite Egyptian tribe has lost the tribal property, yet retained status through deep lineage: "the land had been theirs since the sun first blazed down on the shifting sand" (al-Tahawy 2008, 9).

5. In the mid-1980s when the price of oil plummeted, governments wanted to conserve what looked like dwindling wealth. The first to lose their passports were the `ajam, who, for a while, joined the Bedoon.

6. For Ibn Khaldun, the `arab were socially and ethnically superior, but the `ajam, defined Persians as they are today, were thought to be more creative. Today's `ajam and *haula* would agree concerning their greater creativity (see Melikian 1981, 21).

7. See Davidson 2008, 282–285; Tatchell 2009, 176–178. There is some reluctance today to use the term `abid due to its blatantly racist connotation (conversation with Sulayman Khalaf, Doha, December 4, 2010).

8. Because of their stateless status, figures are hard to establish, but there are approximately 70,000 Bedoon in Saudi Arabia, 100,000 in the UAE, and 120,000 in Kuwait, and "in the 1990s, the Bedoon lost all access to formal employment, health care, and education." http://www.jadaliyya.com/pages/index/6964/an-invisible-nation_the-gulf%E2%80%99s-stateless-communiti, accessed August 23, 2012.

9. http://www.bedoonrights.org/about/, accessed February 20, 2013.

10. On July 7, 2012, the *Kuwait Times* reported that Bedoons had illegally demonstrated against the government, and human rights groups "urged Kuwait government to solve the bedoons issue and end their 50 years of suffering. In a recent statement, rights groups called on the government to naturalize more than 30,000 Bedoons who (the government admitted) deserve citizenship."

CHAPTER 4

1. Although the GCC includes Saudi Arabia and Oman, this book focuses only on the UAE, Qatar, Bahrain, and Kuwait.

2. http://www.uaepm.ae/ar/media/news/articles/news1684.html, accessed June 25, 2012.

3. Robinson later defines hypermodernity as consisting of "an endless flow of re-defined, re-worked and re-structured pasts moving seamlessly towards the inevitable future; a realization of the temporary as a condition of social life...a condition of deeper meanings and closer individual attachment to the world... [hypermodernity] acknowledges both change *and* continuity" (Robinson 2011, 231; original emphasis).

4. http://www.uaeinteract.com/docs/Emirates_Post_issues _stamps_on_Liwa_Date_Festival/50379.htm, accessed July 19, 2012.

5. In 1970, the International Immigration Project of the University of Durham surveyed Qataris' literacy rates: 9 percent aged 60–74; 16 percent aged 30–59; 43 percent aged 20–29, and 78 percent aged 15–19. A 1978 survey indicated an overall literacy rate of less than 50 percent (Melikian 1981, 89). By 2004 the literacy rate had risen to 89 percent, see http://www.state.gov/r/pa/ei/bgn/5437.htm.

6. With thanks to Taieb Belghazi who first drew my attention to the philosophical potential of the *barzakh* (see Belghazi 2001).

7. "Underground aquifers originate from Saudi Arabia and bring sweet water to Bahrain under the sea. There are three aquifers, the

high, medium and the low. Out of these only the medium aquifer contains water usable without treatment" (http://www.al-hakawati.net /english/states/bahrain.asp, accessed October 18, 2011).

8. Ibn Arabi, *Futuhat makkiya*, vol. 3, chapter 369, page 390: "The secret to the special luster of Gulf pearls is probably derived from the unique mixture of sweet and salt water about the island (of Bahrain)." See http://www1.american.edu/TED/PEARL.HTM, accessed March 10, 2011.

9. See http://www.bahrainguide.org/BG1/gardenofeden.html, accessed February 18, 2013.

10. "When Mediterranean Sea water enters the Atlantic over the Gibraltar sill, it moves several hundred kilometers into the Atlantic at a depth of about 1000 meters with its own warm, saline, and less dense characteristics. The Mediterranean water stabilizes at this depth. Although there are large waves, strong currents, and tides in these seas, they do not mix or transgress this barrier... even at places where the two seas were closest to each other, each mass of water preserved its properties. In other words, at the point where the two seas met, a curtain of water prevented the waters belonging to the two seas from mixing." http://www.foundationforpluralism.com/WorldMuslim Congress/PPP/Quran.(mis)translations_031107_091410.pdf, accessed June 24, 2012.

CHAPTER 5

1. http://www.uaeinteract.com/docs/Sheikh_Zayed_in_quotes /18411.htm, accessed November 10, 2011.

2. Kuwait's Abraj, or Towers, with their blue, green, and grey enameled steel tiles recalling mosque decorations that won the Aga Khan Architecture Award in 1980 was one of the first attempts to build a nationally distinct monument that combined traditional motifs with modern usage.

3. The Saudi national museum site refers to the museum as "a cultural and civilization center highlighting the prominent history of the

Arabian Peninsula and its historical message of disseminating Islam."
(see http://www.nationalmuseum.org.sa/introduction.aspx, accessed
June 30, 2012).

4. Contemporary museums' curatorial functions have changed
from primarily interpretative and preservative to experiential and
oriented to a global spectatorship: "The focus shifts to the multiple
meanings of museum exhibits as a result of the changing ideas about
cultural rights, authenticity and cultural authority [the stress turns to]
spectacularization of culture... explicitly oriented to a (global) audience, problematizing their traditional role as sites for rituals of citizenship" (Sassatelli 2012, 238–239).

5. The late journalist Anthony Shadid interviewed an Emirati
woman who wanted to produce a documentary about museums that
she subsumed under the general category of "cultural prostitution."
She threw scorn on these museums and the national obsession with
brands: "Why do we only remember our heritage when it comes to
tourism?" For her, the museum projects were merely about "branding
Abu Dhabi." (Anthony Shadid, "An ambitious Arab capital reaffirms its
grand cultural vision," *New York Times,* January 25, 2012).

6. http://www.tdic.ae/en/article/about-us/whats-new-archive
/zayed-national-museum-set-to-further-raise-uaes-profile-on-the
-worlds-cultural-map.html?view=full, accessed June 1, 2012.

7. http://www.nytimes.com/interactive/2010/11/27/arts/design
/museums.html#foster, accessed June 10, 2012.

8. Nouvel's outpost of the Louvre in Abu Dhabi strikes a different
chord with its Islamic motifs and "a Middle East at ease with technology... Tucked under the dome, the galleries and their watery setting
refer to Venice—an emblem, Mr. Nouvel has said, of the fertile cultural
crosscurrents that once existed between East and West" (Ouroussoff
2010, 3).

9. http://www.designboom.com/weblog/cat/9/view/9593
/jean-nouvel-new-national-museum-qatar.html, accessed October
19, 2011.

10. For an idea of what the museum will look and feel like, see You-Tube http://www.youtube.com/watch?v=MOaw4lYLtOk, accessed January 30, 2013.

11. http://www.designboom.com/weblog/cat/9/view/9593/jean-nouvel-new-national-museum-qatar.html, accessed January 10, 2012.

12. http://www.dezeen.com/2010/03/24/national-museum-of-qatar-by-jean-nouvel/, accessed June 26, 2012.

13. http://www.nybooks.com/blogs/nyrblog/2011/nov/20/islamic-art-doha/, accessed December 17, 2011.

14. The Blue Souq in Sharjah is a similar venture but less successfully rendered, since it is no more than an orientalist shell housing a mall.

15. Qatari men with an undergraduate degree are given a house or an apartment or a piece of land and up to 1.2 million Qatari Riyals (about $330,000 in 2010) toward construction of a house (conversation with Muhammad 'Ali 'Abdullah, Doha, October 10, 2010).

16. Conversation with Marlene Heck, Hanover, NH, May 24, 2012.

17. Conversation with Muhammad 'Ali 'Abdullah, Doha, September 20, 2010.

18. Conversation with Mr. Al Emadi in his Doha home, December 2, 2010.

19. The same search for information from maps, photographs, and archaeological excavation about original walls, buildings, styles, and locations has characterized heritage construction in other Gulf states (Fox, Mourtada-Sabbah, and al-Mutawa 2006, 278, 280, 281).

20. The Qatar Tourism Authority boasts, "the Souq was renovated according to traditional Qatari architectural techniques, using authentic materials. The only traditional souq to remain in the Gulf." (http://qatartourism.gov.qa/pillars/index/1/leisure/267, accessed January 29, 2013).

21. "Their First Lenny Bruce Could Be Coming" (*New York Times Magazine*, May 27, 2012).

22. L. L. Wynn's critique of tourism literature deconstructs the notion that the "commodification of cultural forms…rendered traditional culture inauthentic and therefore meaningless." She argues against theorists who contend that "the tourist and the touristed are locked in a dialectic: authenticity lost and sought, authenticity voyeuristically consumed and thereby eroded" (Wynn 2008, 13, 14). Her analysis of the mutually constitutive encounters between local and foreign questions the very category of the authentic.

23. Jocelyn Sage Mitchell from Northwestern University–Qatar conducted a survey among 798 respondents. She asked "to what extent do the following projects (Suq Waqif, the Museum of Islamic Art, the Imam Muhammad ibn Abd al-Wahhab national mosque, Katara and Education City) represent Qatari culture, values, or traditions?" The outcome: "77% of Qataris say that Souq Waqif and the national mosque (both designed by Muhammad ʿAli ʿAbdullah) represent Qatari culture, values or traditions 'a great deal.'" (Email communications January 29 and February 19, 2013).

24. See http://www.uonbi.ac.ke/departments/arch-build-sci/links /Aga%20Khan%20Award%20for%20Architecture%20Home %20Page.htm, accessed November 9, 2010.

25. http://www.youtube.com/watch?v=y_wxrjhGUGE&feature=g -all-u&context=G23da9feFAAAAAAAACAA, accessed April 2, 2012.

CHAPTER 6

1. Cultural heritage projects are proliferating around the globe in metacultures, that is, "a framework that collects, compares and classifies widely differing cultural manifestations from various periods and various geographical backgrounds…Individuals give themselves and their communities a place on the world stage by means of cultural heritage…Today's global norms are no longer innovation, expansion, emancipation, and the maximization of production and consumption, but rather identity, conservation, and sustainability" (Halbertsma, van Stipriaan, and van Ulzen 2011, 4).

2. Emiratis own falcons in the way that Americans own dogs—lots of them. There is an Emirates Falconers Club that is both social and educational. In 2010, ADACH, the Abu Dhabi Authority for Culture and Heritage Department of Intangible Heritage, inaugurated the International Festival of Falconry and proposed the falcon with its 2,000-year history to UNESCO as an Intangible Heritage of Humanity, and UNESCO agreed (http://www.uaeinteract.com/news/default .asp?ID=72, accessed December 7, 2011). In 2002, the UAE and Qatar gave falcons passports (http://www.ameinfo.com/58497.html, accessed November 15, 2011). See Dubai Ibrahim Mubarak's story "Grief of the Night Bird" in Johnson-Davies 2009, 52–58.

3. In their DIY manual for business leaders, Logan et al. detail the goals of tribal leadership in multinational corporations: "upgrade as many people—and clusters of people—as are willing and able to move forward to . . . the zone of tribal pride . . . While the Tribal Leaders do their work for the good of the group, not for themselves, they are rewarded with loyalty, hard work, innovation, and collaboration" (Logan, King, and Fisher-Wright 2008, 264, 265).

4. In "The Perils of the Pearl Divers," published in *The National*, June 21, 2009, Anna Zacharias interviews an old diver who remembers the anxiety of the men hauling dead divers out of the deep: "We used to wash the body and pray and put the cloth and tie with the rope and throw it in the water." (See http://www.thenational.ae /news/uae-news/the-perils-of-the-pearl-divers#page3, accessed January 25, 2013.)

5. Munif is less critical of the oil than of the way its wealth has been misused: "Oil could have been a road to the future; it could have made possible a natural and continuous progress from nomadic life to civilization . . . but what actually happens is nothing like that" (*Al-Khalij* newspaper, November 21, 1984).

6. See also Bristol-Rhys 2011, 32–33.

7. In the 130 poems, the only references to a life outside the pure homogeneity of the tribal can be found in some satirical poems about Israel (Bailey 2002, 341–380).

8. Some older Emirati women echoed this sentiment: "They bemoaned the new life that had separated them from their memories. 'In the old days, it was better because we were together, we knew each other and we knew ourselves. Now we are strangers in our own land, surrounded by foreigners, letting them tend to our children, and we are prisoners behind the pretty walls of the villas'" (Bristol-Rhys 2011, 123).

9. This image of an old man crushed by tall buildings can be read in narratives from other Gulf countries. Nadia Rahman, for instance, describes an elderly Emirati man looking "at the skyscrapers that define the capital, Abu Dhabi. Perplexed at the glass buildings and large villas that have replaced the original, humble dwellings of a few decades ago, he acknowledges the great achievements, but is still nostalgic for the simple life" (Rahman 2008, 37).

10. In 2011, DFI created a new competition category called "Made in Qatar" and released three films. The following year, nineteen made-in-Qatar films were released.

11. http://www.hollywoodreporter.com/review/black-gold-film -review-259456, accessed January 10, 2013.

CHAPTER 7

1. Lisa Wedeen discusses a similar phenomenon in Yemen, where the repetition of performative practices constitutes individuals and constructs the twenty-first-century nation (Wedeen 2008, 15, 17).

2. Conversation with Zayed University student in Abu Dhabi, December 5, 2008.

3. In her article about the return of the tribal in Jordan and the dialogic relationship between national and local performances of tribal culture, Linda Layne writes about "the changing meanings of the *dilig,* the traditional embroidered dress, for the tribes of the Jordan Valley…In concert with the national valorization of tribal culture, the marked wearing of *dilig* by young women has become a symbol of tribal identity and, by extension, of Jordanian identity…Because *dilug* symbolize "Bedouinness" and, by extension, "Jordanianness," their

selection for wear by young women is a political statement and one that meets with public nods and comments of approval" (Layne 1989, 28–29). The *dilig* is both tribal and modern because it is national.

4. Sara Al Emadi, interview with her father and uncle, Doha, November 5, 2010.

5. Final paper in the tribal modern project at VCUQ, December 2010.

6. In 2010, Islamic banks in the Arab Gulf required its female employees to wear an `abaya regardless of their nationality.

7. In his article about the continued use of *khadi*, or the spun cloth that Gandhi advocated as a return to the true values of Indian society, Dipesh Chakrabarty writes that it is the "site of the desire for an alternative modernity" (Chakrabarty 2002, 64). Although alternative modernities are not the thesis of this book, what is interesting about this statement is the claim to modernity for heritage dress.

8. Nimah Nawwab claims that for some the show "has led to a rise in pride and tribalism," while others lament "the caliber of the work." Nawwab goes on to situate this poetry competition in its historical context: "Pre-Islamic poetry competitions at renowned sites such as *Suq Ukaz* drew poets from all parts of the area as they engaged in poetic battles that often included work composed on the spot" (Paine, Lodge, and Touati 2011, xxiii).

9. In Abu Dhabi there is a street lined with camel sculptures that was recently called Shari `al-Milyun—note the metathesis of the root letters ra and `ain from *sha`ir* to *shari`*. The connection between these two heritage events, the poetry recitation and camel racing, is evident.

10. http://www.bbc.co.uk/news/world-middle-east-17178072, accessed February 28, 2013.

11. Unpatriotic poets pay a high price. German PEN reported that on November 16, 2011, the Qatari state security summoned Muhammad ibn al-Dheeb Al-Ajami to be interrogated about his "Tunisian Jasmine." In this January 2011 poem, he had criticized governments across the Gulf, stating "we are all Tunisia in the face of the repressive elite." On November 29, 2012, he was sentenced to life imprisonment on

charges of "inciting the overthrow of the ruling regime" and "criticising the ruler." On February 25, 2013, the life sentence was reduced to 15 years. http://www.pen-deutschland.de/en/themen/writers-in-prison /aktuelle-ehrenmitglieder/mohammed-ibn-al-dheeb-al-ajami-katar/, accessed March 1, 2013.

12. With thanks to Hissa Zainal for help in finding the poem and then translating it.

13. With thanks to Pernille Arenfeldt for drawing my attention to this notice.

14. Nathalie Peutz, "Revolution in Socotra. A Perspective from Yemen's Periphery." (See http://www.merip.org/mer/mer263/revolution-socotra, accessed June 3, 2012).

15. http://www.movieweb.com/movie/millions-poet, accessed January 21, 2012.

16. "There is a remarkable similarity between the vocabulary of Bedouin Nabati poetry and the classical poetry that was being composed before Islam" said Prof. Clive Holes, the Khalid bin `Abdullah Al-Sa`ud Professor for the Study of the Contemporary Arab World at the University of Oxford. http://www.middle-east-online.com/eng lish/?id=51475, July 10, 2013.

17. In 2012, the Qatari government made Arabic the compulsory language of instruction in K–12 schools and at Qatar University, in order to deal with the problem of illiteracy in Arabic. Despite strong resistance, the policy was implemented in September.

18. http://www.thenational.ae/news/uae-news/education/creation -of-nabati-poetry-academy-prompted-by-success-of-tv-shows, accessed November 27, 2010.

19. http://www.uaeinteract.com/docs/Sultan_opens_Sharjah _Nabati_Poetry_House/34357.htm, accessed November 27, 2010.

CHAPTER 8

1. Rauf Ebeid, "The King was Not Amused." March 29, 2010. http:// www.politicalislam.org/Articles/PI%20573%20-%20The%20King

%20was%20not%20amused%20(4).pdf, accessed November 25, 2010 and http://www.muslimsdebate.com/faces/shownotes.php?notesid=778, accessed November 25, 2010.

2. Her performance went viral, and even America's ABC featured her as the Person of the Week. http://www.youtube.com/watch?v=D55kCS2M7to&feature=related.

3. "78.3 percent of female university graduates in Saudi Arabia are unemployed as well as over 1,000 Ph.D. holders." The Booz & Company report added that since 1992, female participation in the job market in Saudi has increased by three fold as it leaped from 5.4 percent to 14.4 percent." http://www.alarabiya.net/articles/2012/06/11/220016.html, accessed August 16, 2012.

4. Nevertheless, restrictions on women's work outside the home remain so that, for example, a woman in Qatar who chooses to work without her husband's permission may be considered *nashiza* according to family law (Welchman 2012, 389).

5. The Dammam-based Federation of GCC Chambers of Commerce and Industry presented a paper entitled "The Arab Woman and the Global Economy," on "enabling GCC women to support the domestic economy...Independent estimates showed businesswomen in the six-nation GCC control a whopping $385 billion in banks [*sic*] deposits and other investments." http://www.emirates247.com/business/economy-finance/landmark-talks-by-gcc-businesswomen-in-london-2013-03-06-1.497559, accessed July 10, 2013.

6. http://www.reuters.com/article/2011/02/09/idINIndia-54770520110209, accessed November 16, 2011.

7. Sexual, more commonly gender, identity disorder is "discontent with their biological sex and/or the gender they were assigned at birth." It is curious that psychiatrists locate this "disorder," or gender *barzakh* identity, in the *corpus calossum*, a bundle of neural fibers beneath the cortex in the brain at the fissure between the two hemispheres of the brain, where interstitial states like schizophrenia and gender identity disorder are located. http://en.wikipedia.org/wiki/Corpus_callosum#Gender_identity_disorder, accessed September 12, 2011.

8. http://www.src-qa.org/English/DocumentLibrary/SiteDocuments/Publications/Al%20Aween%20Lectures.pdf, accessed July 10, 2013.

9. Conversation with students at the American University of Sharjah on October 31, 2011.

10. Read more: http://www.qatarliving.com/node/953145#ixzz2ourcAM4S, accessed January 7, 2011.

11. al-Nu'aimi, "After the First Thousand" 2001, 79–87.

12. "Al-sayyida al-jalila," in *Abatil* 2001, 101–108.

13. See http://www.sahafa.com/newspapers-and-magazines/Egypt/alahram-alarabi, accessed October 30, 2010.

CONCLUSION

1. http://www.hotelchatter.com/story/2012/7/3/8518/27704/hotels/The_World%27s_First_Harrods_Hotel_To_Open_In_Kuala_Lumpur, accessed December 10, 2012.

2. http://www.guardian.co.uk/business/2012/jul/03/harrods-owners-luxury-hotel-chain, accessed July 3, 2012.

3. http://www.qataruk2013.com/cms/en/about-qatar-uk-3, accessed February 6, 2013.

4. On February 20, 2013, the *Gulf Times* announced, "Qatar, along with Saudi Arabia and the UAE, is increasingly becoming popular as investment destination in the Middle East and North Africa region due to the rise of localised liquidity pools and growing sophisticated collateral and risk management techniques, according to a FTSE global survey."

5. Conversely, international arts are being imported at an amazing rate. Philharmonic orchestras and world class art. In January 2013, BBC announced that Qatar is now spending $1–2 billion a year on importing international art (http://www.bbc.co.uk/news/world-middle-east-20996987, accessed February 2, 2013).

6. Mike Giglio, "Qatar sends aid money to help Egypt." *The Daily Beast*, April 10, 2013.

7. Jodi Rudoren, "Pledge thrusts Qatar into Palestinian fray." *International Herald Tribune,* January 24, 2012.

8. The French *TGV Magazine* for July–August 2012, tucked into the back of each train seat in the country, included an article on Doha's Metamorphosis, and the *British Air Magazine* for the same August period gushed: "Qatar may be the wealthiest nation on Earth but it's not all about hard cash. The state is fast gaining a reputation as the cultural heart of the Middle East with its capital's cutting-edge museums and jaw-dropping architecture."

9. On August 4, 2012, the *Khaleej Times* published an article extolling Dubai's "fine mixing of tribal tradition of authority and legitimacy that the ruler derives from the faith bestowed on him by his countrymen, and forward looking policy shorn of parochialism and narrow-mindedness."

REFERENCES

`Abdullah, Muhammad `Ali. 2010. "Archaeology of Gulf Decorative Styles." Unpublished paper, "Muslim Cosmopolitanism," presented at conference, Doha, December 4.

Abifares, Huda Smitshuijzen. 2005. "Dubai Inc." *Bidoun* 1(4).

Ahmad, Attiya. 2012. "Labour's Limits. Foreign Residents in the Gulf." In *Migrant Labor in the Persian Gulf* edited by Mehran Kamrav and Zahra Babar. New York: Columbia University Press.

Al Ghabban, Ali Ibrahim, Beatrice Andre-Salvini, Francoise Demange, Carin Juvin, and Marianne Cotty. 2010. *Roads of Arabia: Archaeology and History of the Kingdom of Saudi Arabia*. Paris: Louvre Editions.

Al Khalaf, Dana Abdulla. 2010. "Our Changing Language." In *Hazawi: Stories from Qatar*, Volume 4. Doha, Qatar: Carnegie Mellon University.

Al Khalifa, Noof. 2010. "Belongingness." In *Qatari Voices: A Celebration of New Writers*, edited by Carol Henderson and Mohanalakshmi Rajakumar. Doha: Bloomsbury Qatar Foundation Publishing.

Al Kubaisi, Mohammed Jabor. 2010. "Coming to Doha." In *Qatari Voices: A Celebration of New Writers*, edited by Carol Henderson and Mohanalakshmi Rajakumar. Doha: Bloomsbury Qatar Foundation Publishing.

Al Mahmoud, Abdul Aziz. 2012. *The Corsair.* Translated by Amira Nowaira. Doha: Bloomsbury Qatar Foundation Publishing.

Al-Qasimi, Noor. 2010. "Immodest Modesty: Accommodating Dissent and the ʿAbaya-as-Fashion in the Arab Gulf States." *Journal of Middle East Women's Studies* 6(1): 46–74.

———. 2011. "Ladies and Gentlemen, Boyahs and Girls: Uploading Transnational Queer Subjectivities in the United Arab Emirates." In *Circuits of Visibility: Gender and Transnational Media Cultures,* edited by Radha Sarma Hegde. New York: New York University Press.

———. 2012. "The 'Boyah' and the 'Baby Lady': Queer Mediations in Fatima Al Qadiri and Khalid Gharaballi's Wa Wa Series (2011)." *Journal of Middle East Women's Studies* 8(3): 139–142.

Al Suwaidi, Nofe Khalid. 2010. "Social Impact of Globalization on Qatar." In *Qatari Voices: A Celebration of New Writers,* edited by Carol Henderson and Mohanalakshmi Rajakumar. Doha: Bloomsbury Qatar Foundation Publishing.

ʿAlim, Rajaʾ. 2002. *Fatma.* Syracuse, NY: Syracuse University Press.

———. 2005. *Sitr.* Beirut: al-Markaz al-Thaqafi al-Arabi.

———. 2007. *My Thousand and One Nights: A Novel of Mecca* (adaptation with Tom McDonough of *Sidi Wahdana*). Syracuse, NY: Syracuse University Press.

Aljaberi, Jaber. 2008. "Tribal System Promises Much for a New Iraq." February 7. bitterlemons-international.org, accessed March 10, 2011.

Allen, Gregory. 2012. "Tribal Chic. Crossing Borders in Eastern Gujarat." *Journal of the American Academy of Religion* 80(3): 623–658.

Alsharekh, Alanoud, and Robert Springborg. 2008. *Popular Culture and Political Identity in the Arab Gulf States.* London: Saqi Books.

Anderson, Lisa. 1990. "Tribe and State: Libyan Anomalies." In *Tribes and State Formation in the Middle East,* edited by Philip S. Khoury and Joseph Kostiner. Berkeley: University of California Press.

Anscombe, Frederic. 1997. *The Ottoman Gulf: The Creation of Kuwait, Saudi Arabia, and Qatar.* New York: Columbia University Press.

Appadurai, Arjun. 1996. *Modernity at Large.* Minneapolis: University of Minnesota Press.

Arebi, Saddeka. 1994. *Women and Words in Saudi Arabia: The Politics of Literary Discourse.* New York: Columbia University Press.

Arendt, Hannah. 1979 (1948). *The Origins of Totalitarianism.* New York: Harcourt Brace.

Bailey, Clinton. 2002 (1991). *Bedouin Poetry from Sinai and the Negev* (Foreword by Wilfred Thesiger). London: Saqi Books.

Bagader, Abubaker, Ava M. Heinrichsdorff, and Deborah S. Akers (eds). 1998. *Voices of Change: Short Stories by Saudi Arabian Women Writers.* Boulder, CO: Rienner.

Basrawi, Fadia. 2009. *Brownies and Kalashnikovs. A Saudi Woman's Memoir of American Arabia and Wartime Beirut.* Reading, England: South Street Press.

Bayat, Asef. 2010. *Life as Politics: How Ordinary People Change the Middle East.* Stanford: Stanford University Press.

Belghazi, Taieb. 2001. "The Mediterranean(s), Barzakh, Event." In *Global /Local Cultures and Sustainable Development*, edited by T. Belghazi and L. Haddad. Rabat: Publications of the Faculty of Letters and Human Sciences.

Bozdogan, Sibel. 2001. *Modernism and Nation Building: Turkish Architectural Culture in the Early Republic.* Seattle: University of Washington Press.

Bristol-Rhys, Jane. 2011. *Emirati Women: Generations of Change.* New York: Columbia University Press.

Chakrabarty, Dipesh. 2002. *Habitations of Modernity: Essays in the Wake of Subaltern Studies.* Chicago: University of Chicago Press.

Chatterjee, Partha. 1989. "The Nationalist Resolution of the Women's Question." In *Recasting Women: Essays in Indian Colonial History*, edited by Kumkum Sangari and Sudesh Vaid. New Delhi: Kali for Women.

Clifford, James. 1988. *The Predicament of Culture: Twentieth Century Ethnography, Literature, and Art.* Cambridge, MA: Harvard University Press.

Cohen, Ronald. 1978. "Ethnicity: Problems and Focus in Anthropology." *Annual Review of Anthropology* 7: 379–403.

Cole, Donald Powell. 1975. *Nomads of the Nomads. The Al Murrah of the Empty Quarter.* Chicago: Aldine Publishing.

Comaroff, John H., and Jean Comaroff. 2009. *Ethnicity, Inc.* Chicago: University of Chicago Press.

Crystal, Jill. 1990. *Oil and Politics in the Gulf: Rulers and Merchants in Kuwait and Qatar.* New York: Cambridge University Press.

Davidson, Christopher. 2008. *Dubai: The Vulnerability of Success.* New York: Columbia University Press.

Debord, Guy. 1998 (1992). *Comments on the Society of the Spectacle.* London: Verso.

Dresch, Paul. 2005. "Debates on Marriage and Nationality in the United Arab Emirates." In *Monarchies and Nations: Globalisation and Identity in the Arab States of the Gulf,* edited by Paul Dresch and James Piscatori. London: I. B. Tauris.

————. 2006. "Foreign Matter: the Place of Strangers in Gulf Society." In *Globalization and the Gulf,* edited by John W. Fox, Nada Mourtada-Sabbah, and Mohammed al-Mutawa. Abingdon, England: Routledge.

Driss, Hager Ben. 2005. "Women Narrating the Gulf: A Gulf of Their Own." *Journal of Arabic Literature* 36(2): 152–171.

al-Fassi, Hatoon Afwad. 2011. "Saudi Women. Modernity and Change." In *Industrialization in the Gulf: A Socioeconomic Revolution,* edited by Jean François Seznec and Mimi Kirk. London: Routledge.

Field, James. 1971. "Transnationalism and the New Tribe." *International Organization* 25(3): 353–362.

Fox, John W., Nada Mourtada-Sabbah, and Mohammed al-Mutawa (eds.). 2006. *Globalization and the Gulf.* Abingdon, England: Routledge.

Fromherz, Allen J. 2012. *Qatar: A Modern History.* Washington, DC: Georgetown University Press.

al-Ghadeer, Moneera. 2009. *Desert Voices: Bedouin Women's Poetry in Saudi Arabia.* London: I. B. Tauris.

Ghosh, Amitav. 1994 (1992). *In an Antique Land: History in the Guise of a Traveler's Tale.* New York: Vintage Books.

Halbertsma, Marlite, Alex van Stipriaan, and Patricia van Ulzen (eds.). 2011. *The Heritage Theatre: Globalisation and Cultural Heritage.* Newcastle upon Tyne: Cambridge Scholars Publishing.

Hammond, Andrew. 2010. "Television Soap Opera in Kuwait Dissects National Identity." *International Herald Tribune.* October 21.

Hanieh, Adam. 2011. *Capitalism and Class in the Gulf Arab States.* New York: Palgrave Macmillan.

Hasso, Frances. 2011. *Consuming Desires: Family Crisis and the State in the Middle East.* Stanford, CA: Stanford University Press.

Henderson, Carol, and Mohanalakshmi Rajakumar. 2009. *Qatar: Then and Now.* Doha: Waqif Art Center.

————. 2010. *Qatari Voices: A Celebration of New Writers.* Doha: Bloomsbury.

Hobsbawm, Eric, and Terence Ranger (eds.). 1983. *The Invention of Tradition.* London: Cambridge University Press.

Hodgson, Marshall G. S. 1993. In *Rethinking World History: Essays on Europe, Islam, and World History*, edited by Edmund Burke. London: Cambridge University Press.

Holes, Clive. 2005. "Dialect and National Identity: The Cultural Politics of Self-Representation in Bahraini *Musalsalat.*" In *Monarchies and Nations: Globalisation and Identity in the Arab States of the Gulf*, edited by Paul Dresch and James Piscatori. London: I. B. Tauris.

Huesken, Thomas. 2012. "Tribal Political Culture and the Revolution in the Cyrenaica of Libya." *Orient* 53(1): 24–29.

Jaidah, Ibrahim Mohamed, and Malika Bourennnane. 2009. *The History of Qatari Architecture.* Milan: Skira.

Jameson, Fredric. 2002. *A Singular Modernity. Essay on the Ontology of the Present.* New York: Verso.

Jayyusi, Salma Khadra (ed.). 1989. *The Literature of Modern Arabia: An Anthology.* Austin: University of Texas Press.

————. 2005. *Modern Arabic Fiction: An Anthology.* New York: Columbia University Press.

al-Jazairi, `Abd al-Rahman. 1969 (1935?). *Kitab al-fiqh `ala al-madhahib al-arba `a. Qism al-ahwal al-shakhsiya* (The Book of Jurisprudence in the Four Schools of Islamic Law. Section on Personal Status), Vol. 4. Beirut: Dar Ihya' al-Turath al-`Arabi.

Johnson-Davies, Denys (trans.). 2009. *In a Fertile Desert: Modern Writing from the UAE.* Cairo: American University in Cairo Press.

Katodrytis, George. 2005. "Metropolitan Dubai and the Rise of Architectural Fantasy." *Bidoun* 1(4).

al-Kazi, Lubna Ahmed. 2008. "Gulf Societies: Co-existence of Tradition and Modernity." In *Popular Culture and Political Identity in the Arab Gulf*

States, edited by Alanoud Alsharekh and Robert Springborg. London: Saqi Books.

Khalaf, Sulayman. 1999. "Camel Racing in the Gulf. Notes on the Evolution of a Traditional Cultural Sport." *Anthropos* 94: 85–106.

———. 2000. "Poetics and Politics of Newly Invented Traditions in the Gulf: Camel Racing in the United Arab Emirates." *Ethnology* 39(3): 243–262.

———. 2002. "Globalization and Heritage Revival in the Gulf. An Anthropological Look at Dubai Heritage Village." *Journal of Social Affairs* 19(75): 13–42.

———. 2005. "National Dress and the Construction of Emirati Cultural Identity." *Journal of Human Sciences* 11: 230–267.

———. 2006. "The Evolution of the Gulf City Type, Oil, and Globalization." In *Globalization and the Gulf*, edited by John W. Fox, Nada Mourtada-Sabbah, and Mohammed al-Mutawa. Abingdon, England: Routledge.

———. 2008. "The Nationalisation of Culture: Kuwait's Invention of a Pearl-Diving Heritage." In *Popular Culture and Political Identity in the Arab Gulf States*, edited by Alanoud, Alsharekh and Robert Springborg. 2008. London: Saqi Books.

Khoury, Philip S., and Joseph Kostiner (eds.). 1990. *Tribes and State Formation in the Middle East*. Berkeley: University of California Press.

Layne, Linda L. 1989. "The Dialogics of Tribal Self-Representation in Jordan." *American Ethnologist* 16(1): 24–39.

Logan, Dave, John King, and Halee Fisher-Wright. 2008. *Tribal Leadership: Leveraging Natural Groups to Build a Thriving Organization*. New York: Collins.

Longva, Anh Nga. 1997. *Walls Built on Sand: Migration, Exclusion, and Society in Kuwait*. Boulder, CO: Westview Press.

———. 2005. "Neither Autocracy nor Democracy but Ethnocracy: Citizens, Expatriates and the Socio-Political System in Kuwait." In *Monarchies and Nations: Globalisation and Identity in the Arab States of the Gulf*, edited by Paul Dresch and James Piscatori. London: I. B. Tauris.

————. 2006. "Nationalism in Pre-Modern Guise: the Discourse of Hadar and Badu in Kuwait." *International Journal of Middle East Studies* 38(2): 171–187.

Lorimer, John Gordon. 1984 (1915). *Gazetteer of the Persian Gulf, Oman and Central Arabia 1899–1907.* Amersham, England: Gregg International.

Al-Maria, Sophia. 2012. *The Girl Who Fell to Earth: A Memoir.* New York: Harper Perennial.

Melikian, Levon H. 1981. *Jassim: A Study in the Psychosocial Development of a Young Man in Qatar.* London: Longman.

Mignolo, Walter. 2000. *Local Histories/Global Designs: Coloniality, Subaltern Knowledges, and Border Thinking.* Princeton, NJ: Princeton University Press.

Mills, Amy. 2008. "The Place of Locality for Identity in the Nation." *International Journal of Middle East Studies* 40(3): 383–401.

Mitchell, Kevin. 2007. "In what style should Dubai build?" In *Dubai: Stadt aus dem Nichts,* edited by Elisabeth Blum and Peter Neitzke. Bauwelt Fundamente, 143: 130–140. Basel: Birkhaeuser.

al-Mughni, Haya. 1993. *Women in Kuwait: The Politics of Gender.* London: Saqi Books.

al-Mughni, Haya, and Mary Ann Tétreault. 2004. "Engagement in the Public Sphere Women and the Press in Kuwait." In *Women and the Media in the Middle East,* edited by Naomi Sakr. London: I. B. Tauris.

————. 2005. "Political Actors without the Franchise: Women and Politics in Kuwait." In *Monarchies and Nations: Globalisation and Identity in the Arab States of the Gulf,* edited by Paul Dresch and James Piscatori, 204–222. London: I. B. Tauris.

Munif, 'Abd al-Rahman. 1986. *Mudun al-Milh. Al-khandaq,* Vol. 2. Beirut: Al-mu'assasa al-'arabiya lil-dirasat wa al-nashr.

————. 1989. *Cities of Salt.* Translated by Peter Theroux. New York: Vintage International.

al-Murr, Muhammad. 1991. *Dubai Tales.* Translated by Peter Clark. London: Forest Books.

Nigst, Lorenz, and Jose Sanchez Garcia. 2010. "Boyat in the Gulf: Identity, Contestation, and Social Control." *Middle East Critique* 19(1): 5–34.

al-Nu'aimi, Huda. 2001. *Abatil* (Trivialities). Cairo: Al-dar al-misriya al-lubnaniya.

Onley, James. 2005. "Transnational Merchants in the Nineteenth Century: The Case of the Safar Family." In *Transnational Connections and the Arab Gulf*, edited by Madawi Al-Rasheed. Abingdon, England: Routledge.

Onley, James, and Sulayman Khalaf. 2006. "Shaikhly Authority in the Pre-Oil Gulf: An Historical-Anthropological Study." *History and Anthropology* 17(3): 189–208.

O'Sullivan, Edmund. 2008. *The New Gulf: How Modern Arabia Is Changing the World for Good*. Dubai: Motivate Publishing.

Ouroussoff, Nicolai. 2010. "Building Museums and a Fresh Arab Identity." *New York Times*, November 26.

Paine, Patty, Jeff Lodge, and Samia Touati (eds.). 2011. *Gathering the Tide: An Anthology of Contemporary Arabian Gulf Poetry*. Reading, England: Ithaca Press.

Palgrave, William. 1865. *Personal Narrative of a Year's Journey through Central and Eastern Arabia*. London: Macmillan.

Potts, D. T. 2010. "North-Eastern Arabia (circa 5000–2000 BC)." In *Roads of Arabia: Archaeology and History of the Kingdom of Saudi Arabia*, edited by Al Ghabban et al. Paris: Louvre Editions.

al-Qassemi, Sultan. 2012. "Tribalism in the Arabian Peninsula: It's a Family Affair." *Jadaliyya*, February.

Rahman, Nadia. 2008. "Place and Space in the Memory of United Arab Emirates Elders." In *Popular Culture and Political Identity in the Arab Gulf States*, edited by Alanoud Alsharekh and Robert Springborg. London: Saqi Books.

Rahmer, Angelika. 1995. "The Development of Women's Political Consciousness in the Short Stories of the Kuwaiti Author Layla al-'Uthman." In *Love and Sexuality in Modern Arabic Literature*, edited by R. Allen, H. Kilpatrick, and E. de Moor. London: Saqi Books.

Ramsay, Gail. 2003. "Styles of Expression in Women's Literature in the Gulf." *Orientalia Suecana* 51–52: 371–390.

———. 2005. "Symbolism and Surrealism in Literature from Bahrain." *Orientalia Suecana* 54: 133–150.

al-Rasheed, Madawi (ed.). 2005. *Transnational Connections and the Arab Gulf.* Abingdon, England: Routledge.

Robin, Christian Julien. 2010. "Antiquity." In *Roads of Arabia: Archaeology and History of the Kingdom of Saudi Arabia*, edited by Al Ghabban et al. Paris: Louvre Editions.

Robinson, Mike D. 2011. "Meaning in Chaos? Experiencing Cultural Heritage and the Challenge of the Popular." In *The Heritage Theatre: Globalisation and Cultural Heritage*, edited by Marlite Halbertsma, Alex van Stipriaan, and Patricia van Ulzen. Newcastle upon Tyne: Cambridge Scholars Publishing.

Rugh, Andrea B. 2007. *The Political Culture of Leadership in the United Arab Emirates.* New York: Palgrave Macmillan.

al-Saqqaf, Khayriyyah. 1989. "Coal and Cash." *The Literature of Modern Arabia: An Anthology*, edited by Salma Khadra Jayyusi. Austin: University of Texas Press.

———. 1998. "The Loss." In *Voices of Change: Short Stories by Saudi Arabian Women Writers*, edited by Abubaker Bagader, Ava M. Heinrichsdorff, and Deborah S. Akers. Boulder, CO: Rienner.

Sassatelli, Monica. 2012. "Festivals, Museums, Exhibitions: Aesthetic Cosmopolitanism in the Cultural Sphere." In *Routledge Handbook of Cosmopolitan Studies*, edited by Gerard Delanty. Abingdon, England: Routledge.

Schleiter, Marcus, and Erik de Maaer. 2010. "Indigeneity as a Cultural Practice: Tribe and the State in India." *International Institute for Asian Studies Newsletter 53*.

Schofield, Richard N. 1997. "Border Disputes in the Gulf: Past, Present, and Future." In *The Persian Gulf at the Millennium: Essays in Politics, Economy, Security, and Religion*, edited by Gary G. Sick and Lawrence G. Potter. New York: St. Martin's Press.

Shamlan, Sharifah. 1998. "Zainab." In *Voices of Change: Short Stories by Saudi Arabian Women Writers*, edited by Abubaker Bagader, Ava M. Heinrichsdorff, and Deborah S. Akers. Boulder, CO: Rienner.

Sonbol, Amira El-Azhary (ed.). 2012. *Gulf Women.* Doha: Bloomsbury.

———. "The Family in Gulf History." In *Gulf Women*, edited by Amira El-Azhary Sonbol. Doha: Bloomsbury.

al-Tahawy, Miral. 2000. *The Tent*. Translated by Anthony Calderbank. Cairo: American University of Cairo Press.

———. *Gazelle Tracks*. 2008. Translated by Anthony Calderbank. London: Garnet Publishing.

Tatchell, Jo. 2009. *A Diamond in the Desert: Behind the Scenes in the World's Richest City*. London: Sceptre.

Thobani, Sunera. 2007. *Exalted Subjects: Studies in the Making of Race and Nation in Canada*. Toronto: University of Toronto Press.

Tibi, Bassam. 1990. "The Simultaneity of the Unsimultaneous: Old Tribes and Imposed Nation-States in the Modern Middle East." In *Tribes and State Formation in the Middle East*, edited by Philip S. Khoury and Joseph Kostiner. Berkeley: University of California Press.

Torgovnick, Marianna. 1990. *Gone Primitive: Savage Intellects, Modern Lives*. Chicago: University of Chicago Press.

Touati, Houari. 2010. *Islam and Travel in the Middle Ages*. Translated by Lydia G. Cochrane. Chicago: University of Chicago Press.

Trouillot, Michel-Rolph. 2002. "North Atlantic Universals: Analytic Fictions 1492–1945." *South Atlantic Quarterly* 101(4): 839–858.

al-'Uthman, Laila. 2010. *Khudhha la uriduha* (Take her! I don't want her!). Beirut: Dar al-adab.

Wedeen, Lisa. 2008. *Peripheral Visions: Publics, Power, and Performance in Yemen*. Chicago: University of Chicago Press.

Weir, Shelagh. 2007. *A Tribal Order: Politics and Law in the Mountains of Yemen*. Austin: University of Texas Press.

Welchman, Lynn. 2012. "Gulf Women and the Codification of Muslim Family Law." In *Gulf Women*, edited by Amira El-Azhary. Doha: Bloomsbury.

Wynn, L. L. 2008. *Pyramids and Nightclubs*. Cairo: American University in Cairo Press.

INDEX